Snakeopedia

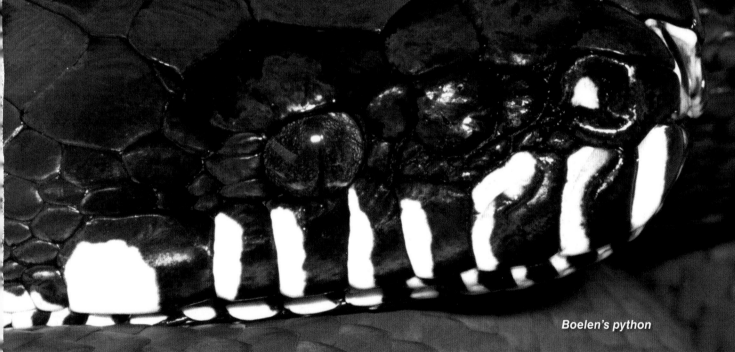

Boelen's python

THE COMPLETE GUIDE TO EVERYTHING SNAKE

With an introduction by Doug Hotle,
Curator of Herpetology at the Albuquerque Biological Park in New Mexico

Time HOME ENTERTAINMENT

Publisher: Jim Childs
Executive Director, Marketing Services: Carol Pittard
Executive Director, Retail & Special Sales: Tom Mifsud
Executive Publishing Director: Joy Bomba
Director, Bookazine Development & Marketing: Laura Adam
Vice President, Finance: Vandana Patel
Publishing Director: Megan Pearlman
Associate General Counsel: Simone Procas
Assistant Director, Special Sales: Ilene Schreider
Senior Book Production Manager: Susan Chodakiewicz
Brand Manager: Katie McHugh Malm
Associate Prepress Manager: Alex Voznesenskiy
Associate Project Manager: Stephanie Braga
Editorial Director: Stephen Koepp
Senior Editor: Roe D'Angelo
Copy Chief: Rina Bander
Design Manager: Anne-Michelle Gallero
Editorial Operations: Gina Scauzillo

Special Thanks: Katherine Barnet, Brad Beatson, Jeremy Biloon, Rose Cirrincione, Assu Etsubneh, Mariana Evans, Christine Font, Susan Hettleman, Hillary Hirsch, David Kahn, Jean Kennedy, Amy Mangus, Kimberly Marshall, Nina Mistry, Dave Rozzelle, Ricardo Santiago, Holly Smith, Adriana Tierno

ISBN 10: 1-60320-990-5
ISBN 13: 978-1-60320-990-8

We welcome your comments and suggestions about Time Home Entertainment Books. Please write to us at:
Time Home Entertainment Books, Attention: Book Editors, P.O. Box 11016, Des Moines, IA 50336-1016

If you would like to order any of our hardcover Collector's Edition books, please call us at 1-800-327-6388, Monday through Friday, 7 a.m. to 8 p.m., or Saturday, 7 a.m. to 6 p.m., Central Time.

Produced by **SCOUT** BOOKS&MEDIA

President: Susan Knopf
Writer: James Buckley, Jr.
Special Advisor: Doug Hotle, Curator of Herpetology at the Albuquerque Biological Park in New Mexico
Editor: Beth Sutinis
Editorial Intern: Brittany Gialanella
Designed by: Andrij Borys Associates, LLC
Senior Designer: Andrij Borys
Associate Designers: Mia Balaquiot and Iwona Usakiewicz
Special Thanks: Leslie Garisto and James S. Harrison

With gratitude to all the passionate snake photographers who contributed to this book. Their enthusiasm and appreciation for snakes and other reptiles, and their commitment to encouraging others—especially young readers—to appreciate these special creatures, is an inspiration.

Eyelash viper gold morph camouflaged among palm fruits

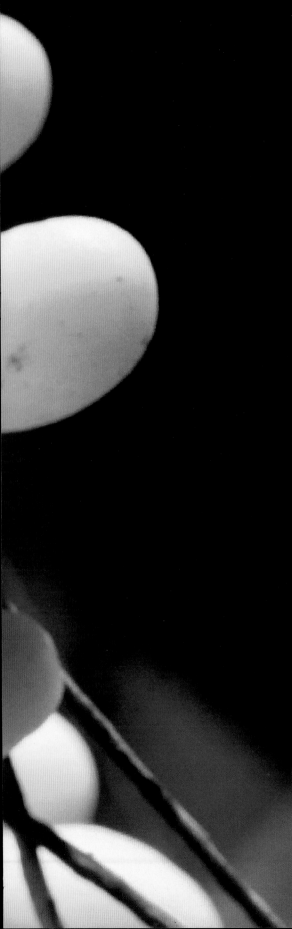

ABOUT THIS BOOK

The group of animals called reptiles includes some of the most exotic, colorful, and bizarre creatures on Earth. In *Snakeopedia* you'll meet hundreds of them.

We start off with snakes. Snakes are among the most fascinating animals in the world. They live in nearly every country and in just about every habitat on Earth. Snakes come in a wide variety of colors, patterns, and lengths, with an array of head shapes, types of tails, and arrangements of teeth. They range from tiny blind snakes that can fit onto a dime to massive anacondas that require a half dozen people to lift. If you think, as the saying goes, that "if you've seen one snake, you've seen them all," think again. The hundreds of photographs in this book will show you just how different and amazing snakes can be.

Inside, you'll read about different types of fangs, how venom works, and the ways in which snakes kill and eat their prey. And you'll learn about constrictors such as boas and pythons. Travel to the rainforest to meet the anaconda or to the Sahara to watch a sidewinder. See how snakes move, eat, give birth, and defend themselves. You'll discover which snakes are dangerous, including a rogues' gallery of deadly snakes around the globe, and learn why we need snakes. Be sure to look out for the section on reptile conservation efforts. Make note of the "FANG FACT," "DID YOU KNOW?" and "REPTILE REPORT" features, which add interesting bits of information. Additional sections in the book about crocodiles, turtles, and lizards will expand your knowledge of reptiles.

Along the way, Doug Hotle will be your guide. He is an experienced herpetologist (snake expert). He has worked with thousands of snakes and brings hands-on expertise to the pages of *Snakeopedia*. Look for special notes from him where you see "DOUG SAYS."

You can read the book from front to back or dip in anywhere—every page is filled with fascinating facts and photos about snakes and other reptiles. Check out "Reptile Taxonomy" and "Snake Anatomy" first and you'll learn things that will help you enjoy the rest of the book. At the back you'll find resources for learning more, including places to go see snakes, other books to read, and websites to visit. Turn the page to begin your exciting reptile adventure.

Contents

"Wally is a day gecko that lives in my office. (A day gecko is a type of gecko that, unlike most, is active during the day.) He is free to come and go as he pleases, but has stayed for more than two years now. For a while he lived on my computer screen because it was warm. Naturally that got annoying pretty quickly. So I rigged up his own private basking spot and he now uses that while he watches me work. Of course, I feed him, so he's got it made."

A rewarding part of curator Doug Hotle's work is talking to visitors about the animals in his care.

DOUG'S FAVORITE SNAKES

Asking me to choose my favorite snake is like asking a father to name his favorite child. But I do have a couple of snakes that I'm very close to. I spent a lot of time researching timber rattlesnakes in the wild. I discovered a lot about them and worked with hundreds of them. Another of my favorites is the mangrove snake. I think I'm the only one in the U.S. who is regularly reproducing them in captivity. I'm trying to get the imported wild snakes out of the pet trade. By breeding captive-born mangrove snakes, we can keep the wild ones in their native habitats.

I'm very excited to be part of *Snakeopedia* and help spread the word to young readers about my favorite animals. Most kids are fascinated with reptiles, and even those who aren't can use this book to learn about how snakes fit into nature. Why do reptiles do what they do? How do snakes help us out? Snakes keep dangerous rodent populations down; they help people in the medical field; they help control fish populations; and much more. Snakes were a part of our planet long before we came along. Every day, scientists discover more about these animals, and with that we learn more about ourselves.

I cannot remember a time when my life did not involve reptiles. When I was very little, my favorite toys were plastic dinosaurs. Before I could actually read, I could name every dinosaur in the books I looked at. At first I wanted to be a dinosaur veterinarian, but I quickly found out that would be impossible. So I turned to the reptiles that are still among us.

I got my first snake when I was eight years old—a garter snake I caught near my neighborhood. During that time I read nothing but reptile books and tried to learn all I could about reptiles. While other kids dreamed of becoming firefighters or astronauts, I decided that I would grow up to become a herpetologist—more specifically, a reptile curator for a world-class zoo.

After many years of reading and study, I've been able to make my dream come true. I wake up every day excited to come to work as a herpetologist and a zoo curator. In my career, I've worked with just about every species of animal you can think of, but my fascination with reptiles has endured. In fact, if I ever get aggravated doing paperwork in my office, I get up and go work with a cobra. I'm more at home with snakes than with most people.

Sadly, scientists say that the future may not be so bright for snakes. Recent studies have shown that all over the world snakes are vanishing. Herpetologists estimate that almost a third of the world's snake species are in decline. There are many different reasons for the decline, but all of them point back to human actions—loss of habitat, lack of prey, pollution, and over-collection for the pet trade. Knowing how snakes and all animals play a part in the natural world will encourage young scientists to make sure the natural world stays healthy.

As students of the natural world, you will find many motivations for learning about snakes, starting with what you'll find in *Snakeopedia*. I get as thrilled today with any snake I meet as I did when I found that first garter snake as a kid. The neat thing about animals is that there is always more to learn about them. This book is a great first step, but don't stop there. We should always keep looking to learn more, and to use that knowledge to shape the future of this amazing planet we live on.

Respect and Protect,

Doug Hotle

Doug Hotle is the Curator of Herpetology at the Albuquerque Biological Park in New Mexico.

The Name Game

Many species of reptiles are known by a number of names. However, the scientific name given to each animal lets scientists know exactly what animal they are dealing with. For example, people in America's Deep South might call one particular snake a cottonmouth, but from Alabama to Zanzibar, scientists know it as *Agkistrodon piscivorus*.

Bloodsucker lizard (Calotes versicolor)

WORD!

The scientific name for the class of animals known as reptiles is **Reptilia** (rep-TIL-ee-uh).

Elongated tortoise (Indotestudo elongata)

Carpet python (Morelia spilota)

Organizing all the animals and plants that exist in the world is a difficult task. There are millions of different kinds of animals and plants that we know about. Fortunately, a Swedish scientist named Carl Linnaeus created a naming system more than 200 years ago. Since then, every newly discovered animal and plant has been named using his system. This way of organizing our natural world is called taxonomy.

SCIENTIFIC NAMING SYSTEM FOR ANIMALS

Kingdom	All parts of the natural world fall into one of three kingdoms: animal, plant, or mineral.	Reptiles are in the animal kingdom.
Phylum (FYE-luhm)	The animal kingdom is split into two phyla (which means more than one phylum): vertebrates (animals with backbones) and invertebrates (animals without backbones).	Reptiles are vertebrates (vertebrates are also called Chordata).
Class	Each phylum is divided into classes.	Reptiles, or Reptilia, are one of the major classes; other classes include fish, mammals, and birds.
Order	Members of a class that share orders: common features are put together in orders.	Reptiles are divided into four orders: Squamata, Crocodilia, Testudines, Rhynchocephalia.
Family	Members with even more similarities are grouped together into families.	Scientists actually argue about how many snake and lizard families there are.
Genus (JEE-nuhs)	A genus includes members of a family that have many things in common.	More than one genus? Say "genera" (JEN-ur-uh). Reptiles as a whole include more than 500 genera.
Species	Each genus is made up of different species.	There are more than 9,500 species of reptiles.

The World of Reptiles

Reptiles are a class of animals that includes four orders. The four orders are Squamata (snakes and lizards), Crocodilia, Testudines (turtles and tortoises), and Rhynchocephalia (tuatara).

SNAKE FAMILY

About 3,500 species of snakes in 21 families live all around the world, on every continent except Antarctica. Scientists divide them into families based on their body parts, but also because of similar behaviors.

Kingdom: Animalia
Phylum: Chordata
Class: Reptilia
Order: Squamata
Suborder: Serpentes
Subgroups: Alethinophidia, Scolecophidia

LIZARD FAMILY

With more than 5,500 species in 27 families, lizards make up the largest branch of the reptile family tree. Like snakes, lizards are found on every continent except Antarctica and in a wide variety of habitats.

Kingdom: Animalia
Phylum: Chordata
Class: Reptilia
Order: Squamata
Suborder: Lacertillia

CROCODILE FAMILY

This small Reptilia family includes alligators, caimans, gharials, and crocodiles, and has 23 species.

Kingdom: Animalia
Phylum: Chordata
Class: Reptilia
Order: Crocodilia

TURTLE FAMILY

Famous for their thick shells, turtles come in a wide variety of sizes. Turtles usually live in or near water, while tortoises live on land. They're all in the same order, though, called Testudines. More than 300 species of these armor-plated animals are found around the world.

Kingdom: Animalia
Phylum: Chordata
Class: Reptilia
Order: Testudines
Suborders: Cryptodira, Pleurodira

TUATARA FAMILY

One of the closest living relatives to dinosaurs is a reptile that gets its own order. The tuatara has only two species in its order, Rhynchocephalia. All the world's wild tuataras live on islands near New Zealand. Scientists think that tuataras have not changed at all in more than 170 million years, and tuataras are often referred to as living fossils.

Kingdom: Animalia
Phylum: Chordata
Class: Reptilia
Order: Rhynchocephalia

Green rat snake

Snakes

From the mighty anaconda to tiny blind snakes, from fearsome rattlers to pet pythons, snakes are some of the most fascinating creatures on the planet.

All snakes are reptiles. Like other reptiles, they are vertebrates (that is, they have a backbone) and have scales. But snakes are different from other reptiles in a variety of ways—often in what they lack.

FANG FACT

Snakes are vertebrates, which means they have a backbone also known as a spine. A pair of ribs grows from each of the vertebrae (parts of the backbone). Those ribs give the snake its roundish shape. And they make the snake's body flexible, so it can undulate (move in a wavy fashion) and curl up.

OTHER SNAKELIKE ANIMALS

Eels are long and thin like snakes, but they breathe through gills and do not have scales.

Worms look snakelike but they do not have bones; they are invertebrates.

A small group of snakelike reptiles are called amphisbaenians. But their scales are arranged in rings, not in rows.

Some lizards do not have legs . . . but they do have eyelids, so they're not snakes.

Compared to many other animals, a snake doesn't have nearly as many body parts. However, snakes have evolved to be exactly what they need to be to survive. Life without limbs might seem hard but for a snake it's just perfect.

▶ Snakes have no limbs—no legs, no arms, no feet. A few lizards do not have legs, but they have other parts that make them different from snakes.

Honduran milk snake

▶ Snakes do not have ears. They "hear" through their bones by receiving vibrations from the ground. They also have an inner ear similar to mammals.

▶ Snakes have no eyelids; they seem to be always staring.

▶ Some snake features can't be seen from the outside. Unlike lizards, snakes use only one of their two lungs; the second is vestigial—leftover from an earlier use—in most snakes.

▶ In snakes, the upper and lower jawbones are only connected by a ligament, which lets them open their mouths very wide to swallow prey. The jawbones of lizards are connected.

Body of the Beast

Snakes all have the same basic body shape—they're thin and tubelike. However, they vary greatly in size, length, color, and even the shape of their head. Check out this butter corn snake to learn about the main body parts shared by all snakes.

Tail

Scales

FANG FACT

This butter corn snake is about 5 feet long. Snakes range in length from pythons that can be more than 20 feet long to a 4-inch thread snake that lives on the Caribbean island of Barbados. The longest snake currently in a zoo is a reticulated python that is 25 feet long.

ANATOMY

Anatomy is the scientific study of an organism—in this case the snake's body—to learn about all its parts. Scientists learn many things through the study of anatomy. Some of the things they learn include how blood flows through the body, how food is digested, how the snake breathes, and where its bones, muscles, and organs are located.

Nostrils

Eyes

Head

Neck

Butter corn snake

TEXAS BLIND SNAKE

Family: *Leptotyphlopidae*
Species: *Leptotyphlops dulcis*

Snakes sometimes have confusing names. The Texas blind snake is also known as the Texas thread snake.

The Texas blind snake is not completely blind—it can tell the difference between shades of light. Blind snakes don't need to see much. They spend nearly all of their lives underground, digging into soil in search of their favorite food: insects.

In the case of the Texas blind snake, that food is mainly termites and ants. At only about 4 inches long and very slender, the Texas blind snake is built perfectly for burrowing. These snakes use a sharp spine on their tail to dig. When they reach an underground insect nest, they use a unique form of disguise. The snake coats its skin with a thick liquid it expels from its rear that prevents the insects from recognizing the snake. Undetected, the snake is free to feed on the unsuspecting prey.

A full-grown blind snake is small enough to fit on a dime.

WORKING FOR OWLS

Texas blind snakes have been seen working with elf owls, as shown here . . . but not by choice. A mother owl snatches up a snake after a rain and deposits it into a nest of owlets. The snake eats parasites that might be harmful to baby birds.

Blind Snakes

Blind snakes are not completely blind, just nearly so. They live almost all of their lives underground. Seeing is not important to their survival, so they have evolved without sight. Using their other senses, blind snakes hunt the insects that live in underground burrows.

SMALL DIFFERENCES

Family Resemblance
It takes an expert (or another blind snake) to tell the more than 200 species apart. The Australian state of Victoria, for example, is home to four similar-looking blind snake species, including this Southern Australian blind snake.

Out-of-town visitor The Brahminy blind snake shown here is native to Southeast Asia. Because people have brought in the harmless snake as a pet, it is now found in the wild in Florida, parts of which have a climate similar to the snake's native home.

STAR SNAKE

COMMON NAME
Texas Blind Snake

SCIENTIFIC NAME
Leptotyphlops dulcis

HABITAT
Desert, grassland

LOCATIONS
Southwestern and midwestern U.S., northern Mexico

AVERAGE LENGTH
4 to 10 inches

FEEDS ON
Termites, ants, and other insects

Small but Amazing

The best place to find the snakes in these families is underground. They are all burrowing snakes that seek their prey below the Earth's surface. The thread snakes of the *Leptotyphlopidae* family are found in North America. The snakes in the *Anomalepididae* and *Typhlopidae* families live in Africa and South America. Most are less than a foot long, though some blind snake species can reach 3 feet long.

FAMILY ALBUMS

When families of animals share many traits, scientists put those families into superfamilies, such as the ones shown here.

Leptotyphlopidae
Thread snakes (top)

Anomalepididae
Dawn blind snakes (middle)

Typhlopidae
Blind snakes (bottom)

DID YOU KNOW?

Nearly all animals need a male and female to reproduce. A few rare species are parthenogenetic (PAR-the-noh-jeh-NET-ik). That means that a female of that species has all the parts needed to make babies and does not need a male to reproduce. The Brahminy blind snake (part of the *Typhlopidae* family) is one of only a few snakes to reproduce this way.

LEFTOVER LEGS

Snakes do not have legs. Prehistoric animals that evolved into snakes did, however. A few snakes, such as blind snakes, thread snakes, and some boas and pythons, have a little reminder of those legs. Tiny spurs, or points, of bone can be found at or just below the skin of some of these species. These spurs are remnants of legs that snake ancestors once had.

Brahminy blind snake

FANG FACT

Snakes in the *Typhlopidae* family are called blind snakes—because they are. They do not see at all, although they can sense light through the spots where eyes might ordinarily be. Since they hunt underground in the dark, blind snakes really do not need sight to survive.

Relatively Speaking

Among snake experts, there is a lot of debate about just how many "families" of snakes should be counted. A family is usually a gathering of animal species that share many similar traits. However, sometimes new information is discovered that moves species from one family to another—or a whole new family gets created. This book describes 21 snake families. Some have only one or two species, while the largest, *Colubridae*, has more than 1,800.

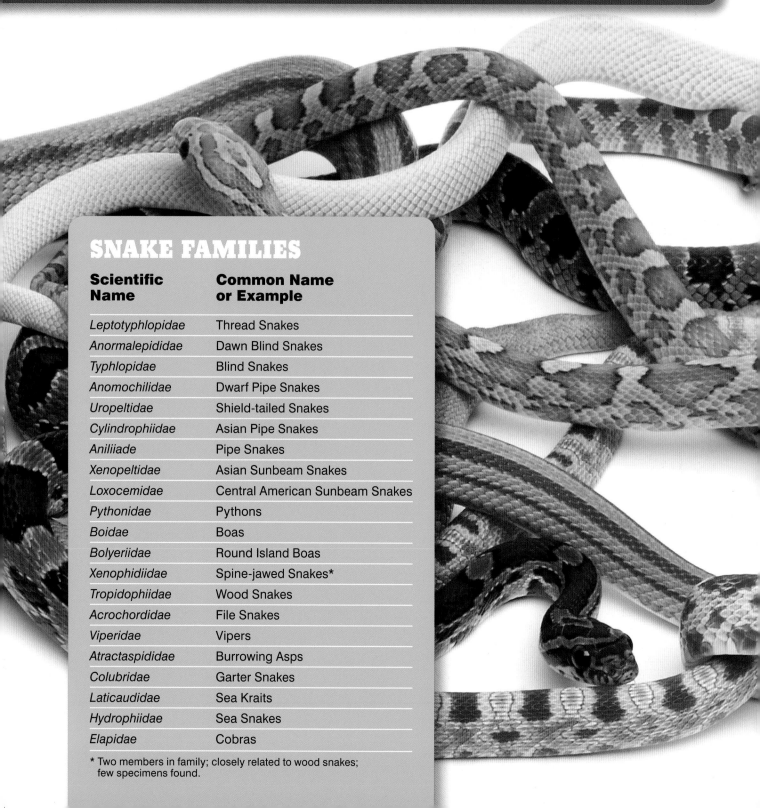

SNAKE FAMILIES

Scientific Name	Common Name or Example
Leptotyphlopidae	Thread Snakes
Anormalepididae	Dawn Blind Snakes
Typhlopidae	Blind Snakes
Anomochilidae	Dwarf Pipe Snakes
Uropeltidae	Shield-tailed Snakes
Cylindrophiidae	Asian Pipe Snakes
Aniliiade	Pipe Snakes
Xenopeltidae	Asian Sunbeam Snakes
Loxocemidae	Central American Sunbeam Snakes
Pythonidae	Pythons
Boidae	Boas
Bolyeriidae	Round Island Boas
Xenophidiidae	Spine-jawed Snakes*
Tropidophiidae	Wood Snakes
Acrochordidae	File Snakes
Viperidae	Vipers
Atractaspididae	Burrowing Asps
Colubridae	Garter Snakes
Laticaudidae	Sea Kraits
Hydrophiidae	Sea Snakes
Elapidae	Cobras

* Two members in family; closely related to wood snakes; few specimens found.

With more than 3,500 species of snakes in the world, organizing them can be a tricky job. Scientists use several methods to put snakes into related families but the experts don't always agree on whether snakes should belong to one family list or another.

TIME FOR TESTING

For many years, snakes were grouped into families based solely on what they looked like, inside and out. If they had similar shapes, scales, or habits, they were in the same family. However, in recent years, DNA testing has been used to be more exact. Scientists have discovered that snakes they thought were related are in fact not related and vice versa.

DNA, or deoxyribonucleic acid, is a chemical that is part of every living thing. DNA tells cells how to build bodies. Scientists learn about how an animal lives and grows by studying DNA.

Scaleless corn snakes, members of the Colubridae family

A snake species is classified as belonging to a particular family based on its characteristics. Many families are very closely related, and DNA evidence may be needed to tell them apart. The green tree python, shown at left, is a member of the *Pythonidae* family, and the emerald tree boa, shown at right, is a member of *Boidae* family. They look very much alike, but looks can be deceiving. In fact, the key differences between these two families are things you can't see, such as the shape and arrangement of bones in their heads.

GRAY'S EARTH SNAKE

Family: *Uropeltidae*
Species: *Uropeltis melanogaster*

The family of shield-tailed snakes takes this name from the way its tail is formed. All of the snakes in this family have hard, flat tails shaped like a disk or shield. They use their tails to burrow into the ground in search of insects or worms to eat. The tails cut through the soil, which is where the "earth snake" name comes from.

The Gray's earth snake has one of the most interesting tails in the family. Rounded and hard as bone, it is also rough as sandpaper.

Like other shield-taileds, the Gray's earth snake has a pointed head. This also helps it push through the soil and poke into crevices where insects might be hiding. Shield-taileds have very flexible necks. The bones of their neck can move much farther and twist more than those of most snakes. Experts think this helps the snake use its head like a shovel, pushing dirt aside and back and forth as it tunnels toward each meal.

Sri Lanka, an island country off the coast of India, is home to 14 of the more than 50 species of *Uropeltidae*.

REPTILE REPORT

This shield-tailed snake got part of its name from John E. Gray, a British zoologist. Gray cataloged hundreds of animals when he was keeper of zoology at the British Museum, including this snake from Sri Lanka.

Shield-tailed Snakes

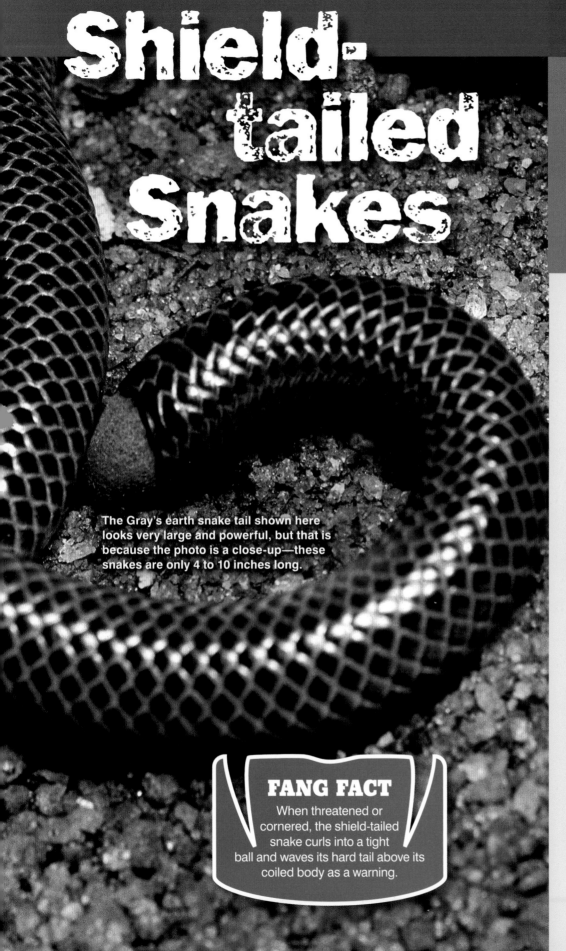

A pointed head and flexible neck help shield-tailed snakes burrow their way into underground homes. The family name comes from the unique tails that every snake in this family has. Unlike those of most snakes, these tails are rigid and hard.

The Gray's earth snake tail shown here looks very large and powerful, but that is because the photo is a close-up—these snakes are only 4 to 10 inches long.

STAR SNAKE

COMMON NAME

Gray's Earth Snake

SCIENTIFIC NAME

Uropeltis melanogaster

HABITAT

Forest

LOCATION

Sri Lanka

AVERAGE LENGTH

4–10 inches

FEEDS ON

Invertebrates, insects, eggs

FANG FACT

When threatened or cornered, the shield-tailed snake curls into a tight ball and waves its hard tail above its coiled body as a warning.

The Tale of Tails

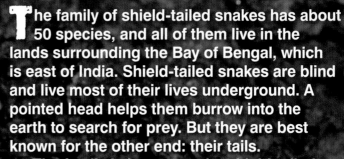

The family of shield-tailed snakes has about 50 species, and all of them live in the lands surrounding the Bay of Bengal, which is east of India. Shield-tailed snakes are blind and live most of their lives underground. A pointed head helps them burrow into the earth to search for prey. But they are best known for the other end: their tails.

The family is known as the shield-tailed snakes because their tails have spines, rough skin, spikes, or hardened plates. Experts think a shield-tailed snake uses its tail to anchor it to its burrow while it feeds, or as a shield to defend itself from other snakes that follow it into the burrow.

SNAKE TAILS

At first glance, snake tails might seem to be all the same: long and slender, usually pointed. But the world of snakes has a world of tails, too. Here are a few close-ups of the different types of tails different snakes have.

Rattlesnake
Makes a rattling noise with tail to warn off predators.

Ringneck Snake
Curls up its tail and shows the bright red underside to scare off predators.

Sharp-tailed Snake
Single spine on tail pins
down prey for eating.

Sea Snake
Flat, thin, rudderlike tail;
used as paddle to move
through the water.

Spider-tailed Viper
Iranian desert dweller; has tail that looks
like spider or centipede. Lures prey to
tail before attacking.

When people think of snakes, they may first think of an open mouth with two fierce fangs. Fangs are long, sharp teeth—longer than other teeth—that are used to stab prey. Cats, dogs, and wolves have fangs at the front of their mouths where they're easily seen. Many snakes have fangs, too, but where they are located can vary from species to species. Scientists divide fanged snakes into three groups: those with hollow, movable, or hinged fangs in the front of the mouth; those with nonmovable front fangs; and those with solid fangs in the back. The hollow fangs inject venom in one swift bite.

Young emerald tree boas are orange; their skin turns green when they are about a year old.

UNLIMITED SUPPLY

Snakes grow replacement fangs. When a fang breaks off or is damaged, another one takes its place. Snakes can grow replacement fangs and teeth throughout their lives.

Pointed fangs are one of the most recognized features of snakes, yet not all snakes have fangs. And fangs are just one of the types of teeth that most snakes have.

FRONT FANGS

Some snakes have front fangs that are fixed, or stay in place at all times. Other snakes with front fangs fold them back into their mouths until they attack. The sharp, pointy fangs of many types of snakes are hollow. Venom flows from small glands in the snake's head into the hollow tooth and is injected into the prey when the snake bites it. The venom kills the prey or stuns it long enough for the snake to swallow it whole.

FANG FACT

Coral snakes and cobras have fixed front fangs that point down all the time. Puff adders and rattlesnakes have fangs that fold back onto the jaw when the mouth is closed.

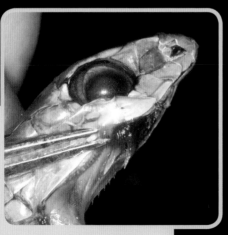

REAR FANGS

Some snakes have fangs near the back of their mouths. Rear-fanged snakes, as they are known, grab their prey with their jaws. The snake's jaw and throat muscles then pull the prey toward the fangs. These sharp fangs are not hollow, however. In most rear-fanged species, the venom flows along the outside of the tooth into the wound on the prey.

PUNCTURE PROOF?

Many rear-fanged snakes eat frogs or fish. These animals sometimes puff up to make it harder to be eaten, but this doesn't always work. The snake's rear fangs can simply puncture these puffed-up animals as if they were balloons.

Not all snakes have fangs, but nearly all snakes have teeth. In fact, many snakes have hundreds of teeth in their mouths. Snakes don't use their teeth to chew their food. Instead, their teeth evolved to make it easier for snakes to capture favorite foods. The teeth curve inward, toward the back of the mouth, to snag prey.

Boomslang snake eating a frog

Expandable jaw of an adult emerald tree boa

OPEN WIDE

Snakes have a big advantage in feeding. They can eat things larger than themselves. How do they do this? Snakes' jawbones can separate from each other to create a very wide mouth opening. After the snake devours the prey, its jaw returns to the normal position.

TOOTHY GRIN

In snakes with many teeth, the teeth run along the edges of the upper jaws, lower jaws, or both. Some snakes have rows of teeth protruding from the bones that run along the roof of the mouth. And some snakes have rows of teeth around their jaw plus teeth on the roof of their mouth. This dentition is ideal for catching and holding prey.

Pythons and tree boas, including this boa constrictor, have two or three rows of teeth.

WORD!

Dentition means the type, number, and placement of teeth. It comes from the same Latin root word as "dentist."

Madagascar tree boa

Many snakes use venom to kill their prey. Venom is a toxic kind of saliva stored in glands behind or below the snake's eyes. Venomous snakes, such as rattlesnakes and pit vipers, inject venom into their prey through or along the fangs. The venom contains various toxins (poisons) that attack different body functions in different ways. The venom immobilizes or kills the prey, which the snake then swallows whole.

A TINY DROP OF DEATH

How deadly is venom? Every venomous species has a different type of venom, and some are more deadly than others. The Eastern brown snake delivers such a tiny, deadly amount of venom in a single bite that dozens of doses would fit onto the period at the end of this sentence. A bite from the largest cobras would be able to kill a person in about an hour. Experts say the venom from some sea snake species is the deadliest of all. Take the venom from an Eastern brown, multiply its strength by 100, and that's what the sea snake puts out.

Milking, or extracting venom from, a cobra in a laboratory.

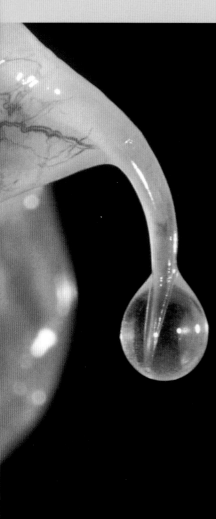

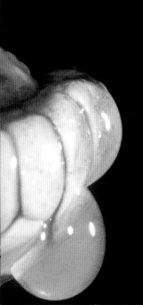

DEADLY NEEDLES

Snakes with hollow fangs at the front of their mouth use them like needles to inject venom into prey. The snake bites down hard and the muscles in its jaw move the venom from glands in its head through the hollow fang and into the animal. Most snakes that kill this way strike their target, inject the venom, then retreat. When the venom has done its work, the snake eats.

DID YOU KNOW?

The same snake venom that can kill people can also save them. Scientists use venom to make antivenom, which acts to reverse the toxic effects of the venom. Antivenom may save a person's life if it is used soon after a bite. Snake venom is also used in medicines that help people with high blood pressure. Scientists are studying venom as they look for cures to diseases such as AIDS, Parkinson's, and Alzheimer's, and even some forms of cancer.

VENOM VARIETIES

The way venom works as a toxin, or dangerous substance, varies from snake to snake.

Venom Type	Effects	Examples
Neurotoxin	This attacks the prey's nerves, so it can't breathe or move.	king cobra, black mamba
Cytotoxins	Cells are the building blocks of all body parts. This type of venom breaks down cells. Body systems fail, and death comes quickly.	rattlesnake, puff adder
Cardiotoxins	This type of venom destroys the heart muscle and blood vessels.	cobra, krait
Hemotoxins	Blood vessels hold blood in the body. This type of venom breaks down blood vessels, causing death.	fer-de-lance

RED-TAILED PIPE SNAKE

Family: *Cylindrophiidae*
Species: *Cylindrophis ruffus*

The red-tailed pipe snake has the widest range of any of the Asian pipe snakes. Living in humid forests or swampy areas, it can be found throughout Asia and Southeast Asia in countries such as China, Vietnam, and Indonesia.

A burrowing snake, it spends most of its life underground. It uses its narrow head to burrow into the ground or follow trails left by other underground animals. This snake usually hunts at night, tracking down other snakes and rodents.

When this nonvenomous snake is attacked, it uses a dramatic defensive move. The red-tailed pipe snake expands and flattens its tail to look like a cobra's hood. The snake then waves this wide tail in the air while coiling itself up. It keeps its head in the center of the coils to make it hard for any predator to reach. The underside of the tail, which faces the predator, has a different color and pattern than the top of the snake.

The pipe snake can confuse attackers by imitating the much larger venomous cobra. At only about 2 to 3 feet long, the pipe snake is no match for large predators, but if they think they're up against a cobra, those predators might leave the red-tailed pipe snake alone.

FANG FACT

The red-tailed pipe snake prefers soft ground near water, where it can spend the day just below the surface. That water is often near populated areas. In fact, pipe snakes risk being run over when they swim or sleep in roadside ditches near farms.

The red-tailed pipe snake makes its tail look like a cobra's hood.

Pipe Snakes

Pipe snakes, as their name suggests, are shaped like a tube or pipe. They don't have a visible break between body and head and are almost worm shaped. They are a rare family, living only in Southeast Asia and South America, and spending most of their time underground.

STAR SNAKE

COMMON NAME
Red-tailed Pipe Snake

SCIENTIFIC NAME
Cylindrophis ruffus

HABITAT
Wet, open lowland

LOCATIONS
Asia and Southeast Asia, including China, Myanmar, Indonesia

AVERAGE LENGTH
Up to 3 feet

FEEDS ON
Other snakes, small rodents, birds, eggs

REPTILE REPORT

The red-tailed pipe snake is found in many different places and was the first snake in the *Cylindrophiidae* family to be named and described. It got its scientific name in 1768 from its tubelike shape (another word for "tube" is "cylinder," SILL-en-der) and its red (*ruffus*) tail.

Pipe Down

Three families of small, slender snakes are all called pipe snakes. Their shape gives them their name. These hard-to-find snakes live most of their lives underground and most live in only a small area of the world, in central South America and parts of Southeast Asia. Though they are burrowing snakes, they have belly scales, which other burrowing snakes, such as the thread and blind snakes, do not have. These scales help pull them through the underground tunnels they travel along.

The Ceylonese cylinder snake is native to Sri Lanka.

NAME THAT SNAKE

Both species of the small *Anomochilidae* family get their name from the people who first found them in the wild. Only six examples of the very rare dwarf pipe snake known as Leonard's pipe snake have been found in Malaysia. It got its name from G. R. Leonard, the man who discovered the first one. The other species, Weber's pipe snake, was named for Dr. Max Weber, shown here, a zoologist who traveled often to the Southeast Asian islands searching for new animals, including the burrowing snake named for him and first described in 1890.

This Asian pipe snake is the only pipe snake found in Sri Lanka. Also known as the Ceylonese cylinder snake, it has a distinctive black-and-white checkerboard pattern on its belly, or ventral scales.

ONE OF A KIND

The South American pipe snake is the only species in the family *Aniliidae*. It often avoids predators using a bit of trickery. The pipe snake's bright orange and black coloring is similar to that of the venomous coral snake, which predators would try to avoid.

Eyes and Vision

Snakes have eyes, but most snakes don't see very well. For example, most animals focus their eyes by using muscles to change the shape of the lens in each eye. This focuses the light and lets the brain "see" what is out there. Snakes, on the other hand, focus by slightly moving their entire eye in or out. This means they cannot focus very sharply on anything. Snakes do see things that are moving—that is, food—better than things that are not moving. With limited vision, snakes rely more on their other senses.

EXTREME CLOSE-UP!

The **long-nosed tree snake** has binocular vision. This means it can use both of its eyes at once to focus. It peers down its pointed snout to spot a potential meal amid the leaves.

The pupils of the **montane slug-eating snake** get bigger at night when it hunts, but the pupil nearly disappears in the daylight.

Like other snakes that lie on the ground and wait for prey, the **gaboon viper** has eyes near the top of its head rather than on the side.

1

2

3

WORD!

Pupil means student, but in this case it also means the black center of an eye. In animals, the pupil can change size to let in more or less light.

Snakes have the same senses that most animals have to gather information about the world around them, and they have some extra senses, too. Snakes use these senses in very specific ways, adapted specially to help them live, hunt, and survive.

FANG FACT

Snakes that are nocturnal hunt at night. They have pupils that look like slits or ellipses. Diurnal snakes, or daytime hunters, usually have pupils that are round. And though snakes don't have eyelids, most species have a single, transparent scale called a "spectacle" covering each eye.

Hearing and Smelling

One of the biggest mysteries about snakes is how they gather information with their senses, but scientists think they have cracked the code. While snakes don't have ears, they have a way of "hearing" by sensing vibrations, and they "smell" with their tongues.

TWO POINTS FOR SNAKES

Snakes do most of their "smelling" with their tongues. When a snake flicks out its forked tongue, it is gathering molecules from the air. The two tongue points then poke into a special place called a Jacobson's organ. Located on the roof of the snake's mouth, the organ sends the information to the snake's brain. This process is called chemoreception. A snake can flick out its tongue even when its jaw is shut through an opening called the *lingual fossa* (LIN-gwel FAH-sa).

EARS TO THE GROUND

Snakes "hear" by sensing vibrations from the ground and the air around them. Special bones and nerves connect their jawbones to their brain. As the snake moves its head along the ground, these bones vibrate in response to sound waves and motion. The snake's brain receives the vibrations and reacts.

SCENT SENSE

The Jacobson's organ got its name from Danish scientist Ludwig Jacobson, who discovered how the organ works in 1811. All snakes and lizards have a Jacobson's organ, and some other animals do, too. When zebras use theirs, they make a very funny face.

GUESS WHAT?

The phrase "speak with a forked tongue" does not mean that the person speaking is a snake. Instead, it means that what the person is saying is probably not true.

Pit Stop

Some species of snakes have another unique way of gathering information about the world around them called thermoreception. Vipers and some pythons often seek live, warm prey. Small organs called "heat pits" on their faces detect changes in temperature, helping them home in on dinner.

HEAT PITS

▶ Pit vipers include a wide variety of snakes, but they get their group name from their heat pits, not from where they live. The heat-sensing organs of pit vipers face forward, one on either side, between the eye and nostril. Many animals use their two eyes to gauge distance; pit vipers' dual pits tell them how big and how close prey is.

▶ Some boas and pythons have long rows of smaller pits on each side of their lower jaw.

Heat pit

Pit vipers can detect temperature differences as small as .002° F. That's two one-thousandths of a degree. For a human to sense a change in temperature, the temperature must dip or rise several degrees.

DOUG SAYS

The Western diamondback rattlesnake, as shown here, is the king of the "heat-seeking" snakes. The Western diamondback is ten times as sensitive to changes in temperature as a python.

—*Doug Hotle, Herpetologist*

WORD!

An animal's ability to detect heat given off by other animals is called **thermoreception** (ther-moh-ree-SEP-shun). This is another way that snakes sense the world around them.

CENTRAL AMERICAN BURROWING SNAKE

Family: *Loxocemidae*
Species: *Loxocemus bicolor*

S nake families can have as many as 2,000 members. The *Loxocemidae* family has only one—the Central American burrowing snake. Because it kills its prey by squeezing and because of the way its pelvic bones are shaped, this snake was once considered part of the python family. However, after scientists learned more about how it lives, they made a new family for it. An animal in a one-species family is called monotypic (mahn-oh-TIP-ik), which means "of one type."

Burrowing snakes are hard to find since they spend most of their time underground. At night they emerge to hunt for lizards, other snakes, lizard and bird eggs, and small rodents. After a strong rain, the snakes may spend time on the surface during the day if their underground homes are damp or filled with water.

To feed, they use their wide, flat, wedge-shaped heads to dig up eggs of other reptiles or unearth lizards sleeping under leaves and soil. They also use their heads and powerful bodies to burrow into the ground.

A long, thick snake, the Central American burrowing snake is a favorite target of larger birds such as owls, so it must be alert while hunting at night.

Sunbeam Snakes

Sunbeam snakes have heads like pythons and rainbow-colored skin, Scientists now separate them to let these shiny-skinned snakes stand on their own, but they did not always have their own family; there are only three species in the group.

STAR SNAKE

COMMON NAME
Central American Burrowing Snake

SCIENTIFIC NAME
Loxocemus bicolor

HABITAT
Forest, grassland

LOCATIONS
Mexico, Central America, parts of North America

AVERAGE LENGTH
3 to 4 feet

FEEDS ON
Lizards, rodents, eggs

FANG FACT
Another name for this snake is the neotropical sunbeam snake. The first part of that name describes the section of the world it lives in—a warm, rainy area that includes Mexico and Central America, the Caribbean, and parts of southern Florida. The second part describes the snake's rainbow-colored, iridescent skin.

A Rainbow of Snakes

Sunbeam snakes get their name from the multicolored shimmer that appears on the skin when it's hit by light. The Central American sunbeam snake is the only snake in its family, and there are only two snakes in the Asian sunbeam family (*Xenopeltidae*). Each is about 3 to 4 feet long.

DECORATIONS

Snake skin comes in thousands of colors and patterns. Along with the sunbeam snake's rainbow style, look for these patterns on snakes.

Blotches
Odd-shaped blobs of color, often with a dark ring around them.

Crossbands
Stripes that go around the snake's back, but not across its belly.

ASIAN SHIMMER

It's too bad that the Asian sunbeam snake (*Xenopeltis unicolor*) spends so much time underground. Its rainbowlike scales are among the most dramatic in the reptile class. It lives only in southern China, Southeast Asia, and on the Indonesian and Malaysian islands. Safe for humans to handle, Asian sunbeam snakes are sometimes captured as pets or hunted for their beautiful skin.

Diamonds
A series of interlocking shapes form a diamond pattern.

Rings
Stripes that go all the way around the snake.

Speckles
Small dots on each scale.

A snake's skin is one of its most recognizable features. The skin is the first defense against disease and injury. Snakes' skin is scaled. The pattern of scales that covers a snake's body is for more than just looking good, however. Scales help the snake move, protect it from enemies, and prevent the snake from drying out.

NOTHING FISHY HERE

Unlike fish scales, which can flake off a fish's skin, snake scales are part of the skin itself. In fact, when a snake's skin stretches, you can see how the scales move apart to show the unscaled skin in between. Not all the scales are the same size and shape, either. Scales form to fit well around each part of the snake's body, such as the mouth, head, and nose.

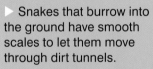

SCALE TYPES

Several types of scales are found on snakes.

▶ Snakes that burrow into the ground have smooth scales to let them move through dirt tunnels.

▶ File snakes have small bumps instead of many overlapping scales. Scientists think these "granular" scales help aquatic snakes grasp fish more easily.

▶ Many snakes have a narrow ridge running along each scale called a "keel."

The stretched skin of a black adder

Spread the word: Snakes are not slimy! Snake skin is usually dry. Scales on the skin help the snake move and feed. And snakes often have bold colors and patterns that help them hide from or warn off predators.

Usually, snake scales lie very close together. The Western bush viper stands out as one that has sharp, raised, pointed scales.

SCALE POLISHING

Some snakes, like this Montpellier snake and a few species of African sand snakes, actually polish their scales. They rub an oily substance from their noses over their whole body. Scientists aren't sure why they do this, but it might have to do with keeping moisture in or leaving a better scent trail.

Changing Clothes

Several times a year, snakes change clothes. That is, they shed the outer layer of their skin, revealing a new layer that has grown underneath. The process is also known as molting or sloughing (SLUFF-ing). A snake can take a few minutes or several hours to shed its skin.

DRESSING DOWN

Snakes start shedding by rubbing their noses or snouts against a rough surface. Then they move their bodies over the ground and the skin rolls off as they move. A thin layer of oil under the old skin helps it slide off to reveal the new skin underneath. The shed snake skin is transparent. A snake's color is part of a deeper layer of tissue that does not come off.

GUESS WHAT?

Snakes shed more often when they are young. Why might that be? Think what a young snake is doing more than an older one—growing. They need a new skin to fit a growing body.

EYE IT

Why do snakes' eyes sometimes look dull or cloudy? When snakes shed their skin, the oily goop that helps the skin slide off covers the eyes briefly and makes them look milky.

*A completely
shed snake skin*

Good Looking!

Snakes are among the most colorful and beautiful animals in the world. Their skin comes in hundreds of shades, patterns, and colors. For some, the color is camouflage, to hide them when they are hunting prey or to warn off predators hunting them. And while most snakes of the same species are the same color, it's not unusual to find variations within a group of snake siblings.

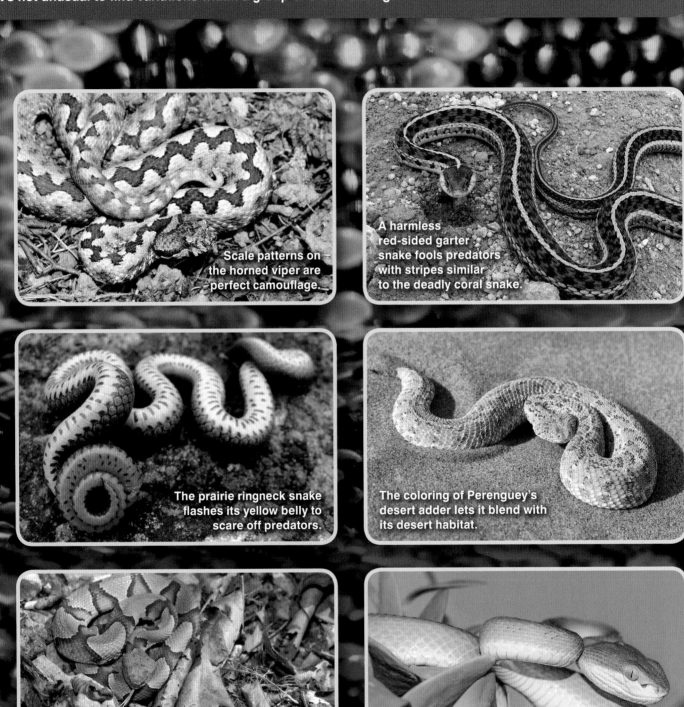

Scale patterns on the horned viper are perfect camouflage.

A harmless red-sided garter snake fools predators with stripes similar to the deadly coral snake.

The prairie ringneck snake flashes its yellow belly to scare off predators.

The coloring of Perenguey's desert adder lets it blend with its desert habitat.

Can you spot the copperhead snake in this photo?

Green scales help the green viper hide amid the leaves.

DOUG SAYS

Being an albino snake in the wild is a death sentence. Without its camouflage coloring, a snake cannot hide itself to ambush prey or to avoid being eaten by predators. The chances of an albino reptile surviving to adulthood are almost zero.

—*Doug Hotle, Herpetologist*

Albino (al-BYE-noh) snakes look white or ivory; they are missing color pigments in their skin. They also have red eyes. Albinos can occur in any snake species, but they are very rare.

FANG FACT

Hog Island boas can change color, getting lighter or darker, very quickly. This helps them hide in the day or night. Despite their camouflage skills, these snakes—popular as pets and overharvested—are near extinction in the wild.

Reticulated pythons are excellent swimmers.

At more than 300 pounds, a python is a handful to carry, even for four people.

RETICULATED PYTHON

Family: *Pythonidae*
Species: *Python reticulatus*

Reticulated pythons, found in Southeast Asia, are the longest snakes in the world. A nearly 33-foot-long snake of this species was found in 1912 in Sulawesi, an island in Indonesia, in 1912, but most adult reticulated pythons are 20 to 25 feet long.

Whether draped around tree branches and hidden among the leaves or perfectly camouflaged on the rainforest floor, the reticulated python waits in ambush for its prey. Striking down from a tree or coming up from behind on the ground, the python encircles its prey with huge coils. After slowly constricting (squeezing) the animal to death, it then swallows it whole. These pythons are so big they can eat entire deer and large pigs.

The species gets its name from its remarkable coloring. The word "reticulated" means "resembling a net." The pattern of lines, colors, and diamond shapes on these pythons looks like a net. This camouflages the massive snake among the trees, leaves, and branches of its habitat.

Pythons

Long, thick, powerful, and beautiful—pythons are among the most recognizable snake species. Living in warm, humid climates, they eat warm-blooded prey. Pythons use constriction to capture their food.

Pythons are closely related to boas. The biggest difference is the presence of two extra bones in pythons' heads.

STAR SNAKE

COMMON NAME

Reticulated Python

SCIENTIFIC NAME

Python reticulatus

HABITAT

Forest, rainforest

LOCATIONS

Southeast Asia, including Indonesia, Philippines, Thailand

AVERAGE LENGTH

20 feet or more

FEEDS ON

Large mammals, snakes, birds

A long with vipers and a few boas, snakes in the *Pythonidae* family have heat pits. These special organs are tiny holes on the face that can sense incredibly small changes in temperature. The presence of an animal can raise the surrounding temperature enough for the snake to detect it. Once it senses the warmth of an animal, a snake with heat pits knows when and where to strike.

THEY'RE THE PITS

A python's pits may be located on the snake's rostrum, or snout, and along the lower jaw. To find them, look for a series of small indentations usually more lightly colored than the nearby scales or skin. Not all pythons have pits, but most do. Heat pits are clearly visible on an adult python, and you can even spot them on a baby python if you look closely.

THE LONG AND THE SHORT OF IT

Among the more than 50 python species, not all are as huge as the 20-foot-plus reticulated python, which is not only the longest python but the longest snake species in the world. The anthill python shown above—the smallest member of the python family—is only about 2 feet long. Contrary to what its name suggests, the anthill python most often eats termites, not ants.

HOT AIR

Most snakes that eat birds attack while the birds are resting in nests. The green tree python works harder than that. Hanging loosely from a branch in its Asian forest habitat, it is camouflaged among the vines. When a bird flies by, the snake senses it using its heat pits, then snatches the bird in midair. To help in this endeavor, the green tree python has longer teeth at the front of its mouth. These teeth can penetrate bird feathers so the snake can get a good grip and secure its meal.

Reticulated python

Pythons are one of the best-known types of snakes. Usually long and thick, they earned some of their fame due to their size and their amazing range of skin patterns. Though many are large, some species of pythons are popular pets.

Most carpet python species live in Australia, though a few also live in Indonesia and Southeast Asia.

Children's Python Native to Australia, this snake did not get its name from kids, but from a scientist. It was named in honor of John George Children, a British naturalist who lived in the 19th century.

Carpet Python You might look at a dozen carpet pythons and think they're all from different species; their colors and patterns can vary widely.

HAVING A BALL

The ball python is considered one of the most popular types of snakes to keep as a pet. Captive ball pythons grow to about 4 to 5 feet long. They can live in a large glass tank with a secure top. Pythons like to have water to soak in, so there should be a large dish or tray in the tank. The ball python also needs a place to curl up and hide as it would do in the wild. Pet owners feed these snakes mice or rats.

Nearly all snakes hunt live animals for food. They kill their prey using venom or constriction (squeezing). Some combine the two, but usually it's one or the other. Very small prey—insects, small rodents, or small lizards, for example—are just grabbed and swallowed alive.

DEATH BY CONSTRICTION

Snakes such as boas, pythons, and corn snakes use powerful muscles to grab and envelop prey. They twist their long bodies several times around the prey and squeeze. It may look as though the animal is being crushed by the snake, but the tight coils actually keep the prey from breathing and it suffocates. When the prey has died, the snake then swallows it whole, usually starting with the head so the limbs fold along the body, allowing for easier consumption.

WORD!
Constrict means to squeeze or compress. Snakes that kill this way are called constrictors.

Snakes are good hunters and have bodies adapted to hunting, killing, and eating their prey. They are carnivores, which means they eat other animals. Snakes have only their mouths and their powerful bodies to capture, kill, and eat what they need.

DEATH BY VENOM

About 600 snake species kill by injecting venom into their prey. These snakes, which have front fangs, usually will strike, inject venom, and then retreat. The venom goes to work, and when the animal is dead or immobilized, the snake begins the swallowing process. Most types of venom also begin to break down the cells of the animal so the snake can digest it. Snakes with fangs in the back of their mouth grab and hold on with their whole mouth, allowing the venom to enter the animal and paralyze it.

DOUG SAYS

Snakes that use venom to kill their prey are considered to be more "modern" than others. This is by far the safest method for a snake to secure its food. Constrictors in the wild will have numerous scars on their bodies from their prey's attempts to escape.

—*Doug Hotle, Herpetologist*

After a snake has killed or captured its prey, it needs to eat the prey to take in the nutrients. But most snakes don't have jaws and teeth that are able to chew food and break it into smaller pieces. To digest the animal in order to get what its body needs, the snake has to swallow the entire animal whole.

EGG-EATERS

East African egg-eaters and Indian egg-eaters specialize in eating the eggs of birds or other reptiles. They completely swallow the entire egg, then break the shell inside their bodies. After digesting the inside of the egg, the snake ejects the broken shell from its mouth. Egg-eaters are the only known snakes that do not have teeth.

FANG FACT

How does a snake breathe with an animal stuck in its throat? Snakes breathe during swallowing by pushing the windpipe to the front of the mouth. This allows the mouth to open wide to engulf prey while continuing to let air pass in and out.

Some very large species of boas and pythons can swallow an entire deer, antlers and all. The neck expands to allow it through.

OPEN WIDE

A snake's jawbone is specially shaped to allow it to open extremely wide. The lower and upper jaws can spread far apart. The snake spreads its mouth completely around the prey and then uses its teeth, jaws, and powerful, body-long muscles to pull the entire animal into its stomach.

REPTILE REPORT

The boa constrictor is one of the most popular types of pet snake. Boa owners must have strong stomachs. Pet boas need to be fed with small rodents, which can be bought frozen at pet stores.

WORD!

When a snake has swallowed something large, its body bulges into the shape of the animal it ate. The normally slender snake shape is **distended** into another form.

Boas

Some of the world's largest snakes are in the *Boidae* family. The powerful members of this family use their strong muscles to capture and squeeze prey before swallowing it. They live in warm areas, often near water, and have a wide variety of scale colors and patterns.

STAR SNAKE

BOA CONSTRICTOR

Family: *Boidae*
Species: *Boa constrictor*

Also called the common boa, this species is best known by its scientific name, which describes its method of killing. The boa constrictor lives in Central and South America and on some Caribbean islands. It has one of the widest ranges of any type of large snake. The coloring of boa constrictors varies from place to place, but all have patches of light and dark on their skin that help them hide among the trees. They also spend time on the forest floor.

Though the boa constrictor is only about 14 feet long and 60 pounds, it has a much bigger reputation. Popular as pets, boa constrictors have long been feared more than they should be. They do not attack humans, and though their bite can be painful, it is not deadly.

The boa constrictor's bite comes in handy for grabbing the rodents, birds, and bats that it eats. After lying in wait for prey to come by, the snake snatches the prey in its powerful jaws. Then it squeezes, or constricts, the animal by coiling around it until the prey stops breathing. After eating the prey whole, the boa might take four or five days to fully digest the animal. During this time, the snake is distended until the prey is broken down by strong stomach acids and digested.

COMMON NAME

Boa Constrictor

SCIENTIFIC NAME

Boa constrictor

HABITAT

Rainforest, riverside, grassland, woodland

LOCATIONS

Mexico, Central America, South America

AVERAGE LENGTH

6 to 14 feet

FEEDS ON

Small mammals, birds, reptiles

Boas and pythons are closely related. But they make up two different families of snakes. From the outside, they look similar: usually very long and rather thick with a wide variety of scale colors and patterns. However, they are different in several ways. Boas lack a group of extra teeth that pythons have, plus boas have a different group of skull bones. Also, under their tails, boas have a single row of scales, while pythons have two. There are more than 40 species of boas living in tropical and arid areas around the world. Boas are found in several different habitats.

Ground boas are shorter than tree boas in general, with thicker, heavier bodies. They live on forest floors for the most part. Their scale patterns act as camouflage for burrowing into leaves, fallen branches, or even coconut husks. The rainbow boa is one of the most beautiful of the ground boas, with shimmering scales.

UP IN THE TREES, DOWN ON THE GROUND

The emerald tree boa spends nearly all of its life in the trees, making it an arboreal snake. The boa's color helps it blend in and a slender body helps it move among the branches. Like monkeys, these boas have a prehensile tail, which means the tail can be used to grasp things such as tree branches.

SANDY SNAKES

The rough-scaled sand boa lives in India, and its cousin the East African sand boa finds a home in Somalia and Eritrea. Only 2 to 3 feet long, the various sand boas track lizards or birds or burrow into the ground to find prey.

WORD!

Arboreal means having to do with trees. In this case, it means animals that live on tree branches and in treetops.

BABY BOAS

Another way that pythons and boas differ—boas give birth to live babies, while pythons lay eggs that later hatch. A large female boa can give birth to dozens of babies in a single litter.

The *Boidae* family includes the largest and heaviest snake in the world: the amazing green anaconda (*Eunectes murinus*). At an average length of 20 feet, it is not as long as the record-setting reticulated python, but the anaconda is much heavier. An anaconda can weigh as much as 500 pounds. Its body can be as much as a foot thick.

HOME IN THE WATER

These heavy snakes cannot move very quickly on land. But once in the water, they swim smoothly and easily. Anacondas live in swamps and marshes in South America. They hunt by gliding up to prey, often at the water's edge. The snake's nostrils are on the top of its head. This lets the anaconda stay almost fully underwater until it's time to strike.

Some people say the Amazon River, the second longest river in the world, resembles an anaconda. What do you think?

SMALLER COUSIN

The yellow anaconda weighs in at about 50 to 70 pounds and is about 11 to 14 feet long. This snake, also known as the Paraguayan anaconda, is native to South America, where it lives mainly in or near water.

Snakes that move in more of a straight line use what is called rectilinear (rek-tih-LINN-ee-er) motion. To do this, a snake moves the muscles along its belly, pushing up and down in a wave pattern. As each section of scaled skin on its belly grips the ground, the body moves forward. The snake's body stays mostly straight using this motion. Heavier snakes such as boas and pythons move this way.

SLITHERING

Serpentine (winding or turning) is the most common type of snake motion. A snake slithering in a serpentine fashion moves its body in sections, back and forth. It pushes against any part of the ground it can, taking advantage of every bump, rock, stick, and root. A snake moving this way looks like a series of S-shaped curves. Tree snakes move this way to climb through branches, too.

CONCERTINA

After moving its head forward, a snake using the concertina method pulls the rest of its body toward the head, forming a series of curls. Then it pushes until the curls straighten, advancing its head and body forward. Burrowing snakes use this concertina motion. Some burrowing species also have hardened snouts or tails to help dig through the earth.

REPTILE REPORT

The belly (or ventral) scales on a snake actually help it grip the ground as it moves. Some snakes can also push out their scales to help grip tree bark, which allows them to climb almost straight up.

Snakes don't have arms or legs, but they do have their own way of moving around. Each species uses the type of locomotion, or movement, that works best in its habitat.

SIDEWINDER

The soft sands of the desert make moving difficult for a snake using rectilinear or serpentine motion. So some desert dwellers, such as the sidewinder rattlesnake and Saharan horned viper, use a sidewinder motion. They slither back and forth, but move sideways instead of forward. By using parts of their body to push against the sand, they are able to move quickly, though it looks at first like they're going in the wrong direction. This also helps them keep as much of their body as possible off the scorching hot sand.

Some habitats or environments call for specialized types of snake movement. Snakes that live underwater have evolved to thrive in their habitats.

UNDERWATER SNAKES

Most sea snakes move underwater with a serpentine motion, but they have an added tool in their arsenal: a flat tail that they use like a paddle. The snakes flick it back and forth, much like a fish uses its tail.

Some snakes glide along the surface of the water, and others swim underwater. They swim by undulating—moving in a wavy motion—to propel their bodies forward.

Sea kraits are venomous snakes that have evolved to live in the sea. Their lungs run the length of their bodies. This lung helps them dive deep and stay under longer. They come to the surface to breathe.

Sea kraits aren't always swimming; sometimes they come ashore to rest on the beach.

Northern water snakes live in or near freshwater habitats. They are found across much of the United States, most commonly in the lakes, ponds, and rivers of the Northeast and Midwest.

Banded sea snake

CUBAN WOOD SNAKE

Family: *Tropidophiidae*
Species: *Tropidophis melanurus*

For many years, this snake was known as the Cuban dwarf boa. Along with other similar snakes, it was thought to be part of the larger boa (*Boidae*) family. But further study revealed that wood snakes should make up their own family, due mostly to the way their lungs connect to their trachea, or windpipe. Little things can mean a lot when determining how a snake fits into a family.

Cuban wood snakes spend most of their lives on the forest floor, hiding among logs, leaves, tree trunks, and roots. They eat as boas do, by squeezing their prey before swallowing. Their main prey includes frogs, birds, and lizards. To attract this prey, the snake will sometimes curl into a ball and leave its light-yellow tail dangling as a lure.

It is on defense, however, that this snake is a star. When threatened, it can squeeze blood from its eyes and nose to scare off an attacker. It can also send out an unpleasant odor from its rear, or, as it's known to scientists, its cloaca (kloh-EY-kuh). As a way to avoid being attacked, the Cuban wood snake can change its skin color slightly as the sun sets, darkening from its daytime bright orange, to hide in the night.

REPTILE REPORT

Cuba has no venomous snakes. The constricting snakes, like the Cuban wood snake, do not bother with people. But they do like to eat lizards, frogs, and birds.

Wood Snakes

A small family that used to be part of the *Boidae*, wood snakes resemble boas but are usually smaller. They also have a different arrangement of lungs. Wood snakes are constrictors like boas; that is, they squeeze prey to death before eating.

STAR SNAKE

COMMON NAME
Cuban Wood Snake

SCIENTIFIC NAME
Tropidophis melanurus

HABITAT
Forest, woodland, grassland

LOCATION
Cuba

AVERAGE LENGTH
30 to 40 inches

FEEDS ON
Lizards, amphibians, birds

The island of Cuba has 15 species of wood snake, all part of the *Tropodophis* genus. The orange Cuban wood snake shown here is the largest of them. Others have more muted colors of brown or gray.

That's Just Confusing!

When is a boa not a boa? When it's a wood snake. The common name for many of the 25 species in the *Tropidophiidae* family includes the word boa. The whole family is sometimes called West Indian boas. But these snakes are not boas from the *Boidae* family.

WHY THE CONFUSION?

Wood snakes look similar to smaller members of the boa family. When discovered, they were first named for those well-known snakes. As scientists studied further, however, they learned more about the wood snake. They found a third, or tracheal, lung that boas do not have. ("Trachea" means "windpipe," a tube connected to the lungs.) So wood snakes became their own family. The wood snake's common name comes from the snake's habitat, which is most often the floor of temperate or subtropical forests.

BOA VS. BOA

Can you tell which boa is from the wood snake family and which is from the boa family?

 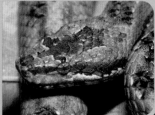

Answer: The wood snake family boa is on the right.

BY ANY NAME, IT'S THE SAME

One of the wood snakes that live in Central America has more than one common name. It earned the name banana boa not because of its color, but because when ships carried bananas to Europe or North America, these snakes were often found mixed in with the fruit. Also known as the bromeliad boa, this iridescent member of the wood snake family is seen at left on a colorful bromeliad (broh-MEH-lee-ad) plant.

A wide mouth springs open . . . a pair of fierce fangs spring into action . . . powerful muscles launch an ultimate predator toward the target. The death-delivering strike of a venomous snake is one of nature's most devastating weapons. Snakes use several methods to get in position to make the kill.

BIG AND SNEAKY

Larger, slow-moving snakes often lie in wait. When prey comes by, they suddenly spring into action, biting hard to inject venom or encircling to use constriction power. This kind of attack calls for patience and good camouflage. Such snakes often wait on forest floors among the leaf litter on the ground. Some may wait for days or weeks for prey to pass by. This is called ambush hunting.

Gaboon viper

CHASE 'EM DOWN

Snakes such as the well-named racer shown here, along with others including whipsnakes and some sand snakes, are active hunters. They seek out fast-moving prey—lizards, small rodents, frogs—and use their even faster-moving bodies to chase them down.

For most of its life, a snake is either looking for food or trying to avoid becoming something else's meal. Snakes attack their prey using a variety of techniques. And they depend upon a wide choice of defense strategies.

THE STRIKE

When striking with its fangs, a snake keeps most of its body on the ground. It shoots its long neck out, leading with its head and open mouth. Some snakes can strike prey as far away as half their body length.

Defense

While snakes are successful hunters, they can also be the hunted. Birds, mammals, and many snakes include snakes in their diet. Snakes have a wide range of defenses against these attacks.

COLOR DISTRACTIONS

Ringneck and red-bellied snakes are among those that can put on a show when they are threatened. If a predator flips the snake over, they get a surprise. The snake's bright red belly scales can scare away a potential enemy.

HIDE

Other than simply escaping, camouflage is a snake's best defense strategy. Sand snakes have the coloring of the dirt and sand around them. Snakes that live on forest floors have speckles or blotches that blend in with leaves and sticks. Tree-dwelling snakes can be one or more of various shades of green that blend with green leaves and moss.

CURL UP

Larger, thicker snakes can fend off attack by rolling into a big ball. The snake puts its head in the middle of this large mass, making it hard for an enemy to reach. The ball python gets its name from this defensive behavior.

WORD!
Intimidation means to frighten or scare without physical contact.

Ringneck snake

GET BIG
Sometimes an enemy can be scared off by a show of size. Several snake species can make their heads look bigger and more menacing. The cobra's hood (below) is the best known example of this kind of intimidation. The puff adder can inflate its entire body with air. The boomslang snake spreads its neck to reveal brightly colored scales.

PLAY DEAD
Some snakes simply play dead. The best at this are the American hognose snake at right and the European grass snake. They flop their heads back, leave their mouths open, and lie perfectly still. Attackers looking for live prey don't want to eat a dead snake.

JAVAN FILE SNAKE

Family: *Acrochordidae*
Species: *Acrochordus javanicus*

The Javan file snake spends its whole life in the water, but it's not a fish. This snake, like mammals such as dolphins and whales that live in water, has to breathe air. As it hunts throughout Asia's tropical waters, the Javan file snake holds its breath underwater. It surfaces and breathes before heading back down to go on hunting. Javan file snakes spend most of their time in the shallow, brackish water near coastlines.

The largest of the three species in this small family of snakes, the Javan file snake, can be as long as 8 feet. This snake has several common names. It earned one, the elephant trunk snake, because its sleek, gray-black skin becomes baggy when it is out of the water. The bumplike scales on its skin are the reason it's also known as a wart snake. Those bumps have a purpose; they help the snake grab hold of slippery prey. After snagging a fish or frog with its mouth, the Javan file snake winds around the animal. The rough skin grips the prey and prevents it from escaping before it is suffocated.

HOLD YOUR BREATH!

File snakes lie in wait for fish and other watery treats. They hide underwater, on or near the bottom, until something swims by. One study found a file snake could stay submerged for as long as two hours without breathing.

File Snakes

The three species that are part of *Acrochordidae* spend nearly all their lives in the water. Their bodies are heavy and awkward, so they have trouble moving on land. Nostrils high on file snakes' heads help them breathe even when nearly submerged.

STAR SNAKE

COMMON NAME
Javan File Snake

SCIENTIFIC NAME
Acrochordus javanicus

HABITAT
River, pond, brackish pool

LOCATIONS
Indonesia, Malaysia, Thailand, and nearby countries

AVERAGE LENGTH
5 to 8 feet

FEEDS ON
Fish and frogs

DID YOU KNOW?

The interesting skin of the file snake is attractive to another predator—Homo sapiens (human beings). This type of snake is hunted in Sumatra, Malaysia, and Thailand for its skin. The skin is harvested and turned into clothing and luggage, among other things.

Hidden Among the Trees

For a snake, a tropical forest can be a perfect place to live. There are hundreds of types of animals to eat there, including rodents, birds, and lizards. There are many places for a snake to hide among leaves, branches, and trees. Snakes in tropical forests have evolved to make use of these natural advantages.

WARM AND TOASTY

The hot, humid tropical forests of the world are home to an enormous number of snake species. Snakes live in the trees, on the forest floor, and even in the cooler, moist soil beneath the trees. Tropical forests are found in South America, Southeast Asia, and central West Africa. These forests surround mighty river systems, providing even more habitat opportunities for snakes.

The green scales of the hairy bush viper flare out to create a very bristly look. The points of the scales help the snake move through trees and bushes, but also help it blend into its leafy forest home.

The skin patterns on the gaboon viper help it blend in with the leaves that cover the forest floor in Brazil and other South American countries.

In Southeast Asia and the Philippines, the mangrove snake is one of the largest and fiercest predators. The forest floor and low trees provide cover for its attacks on rodents, birds, and other snakes.

Trees, deserts, or underwater: these are examples of habitats—areas where a type of animal usually lives. Snakes live in a variety of habitats, most of which are in a wide band on the Earth above and below the equator. That's where temperatures are warmest. Reptiles, such as snakes, get their body heat from the sun and warm air of their habitat.

SNAKE OR VINE?

Tropical forest trees provide a habitat for snakes. The green tree viper poses as a long branch or vine until prey comes by and then it attacks. Look for this species resting at the highest point of a tree.

DOUG SAYS

The rainforests around the Amazon River in South America are home to hundreds of snake species. More and more of the rainforest is being cut down for logging and farms. That means snakes have lost their habitats. Biologists fear some species have already disappeared.

—*Doug Hotle, Herpetologist*

Sand and Grass

The hot, dry desert does not provide many safe hiding places. But by squeezing into any space under a rock, in a small burrow, or in a crevice, a snake that lives in the desert can avoid becoming overheated and try to escape a predator. Also, a snake's ability to move quickly in the shifting sands helps it chase food and avoid being caught.

North American deserts are home to several species of rattlesnake. Their skin patterns blend into the desert landscape. This helps them hide while they lie in wait for approaching prey.

Africa's enormous Sahara is a harsh environment for living. But two sidewinder species have thrived there, using the unusual side-slithering locomotion to get around on the hot sand.

DIG DOWN DEEP

Some families of snakes include species that burrow, such as blind snakes and stiletto snakes. Burrowing snakes often look like worms and have heads that are pointed or tapered to make digging easier. These snakes spend most of their life underground. Some have protective scales on their noses or tails to aid in digging through soil.

WORD!

Burrow can be a noun or a verb. A burrow is an underground space in which an animal lives. To burrow means to dig or live in a burrow, as blind and stiletto snakes do.

SNAKES IN THE GRASS

Snakes can move undetected through the tall grass and shrubbery of grasslands. Without tall trees blocking the sun, more low-lying vegetation can grow. The European grass snake and hognose and racer snakes in North America thrive in such grasslands.

Dozens of snake species make their homes in the waters of the world. They are not fish, however, and must breathe air. Their nostrils are usually near the top of their heads so they can "snorkel" at the surface. However, some have evolved so they can remain underwater for an hour or more at a time.

THE CASE OF ISLAND SNAKES

Snakes that live on islands evolved differently from snakes on the mainland. For instance, they can grow bigger than mainland relatives. An example is the Chappell Island tiger snake, living near Australia, which is the biggest type of tiger snake. It eats only seabird chicks, which hatch in the spring. This tiger snake needs to be big enough to eat a lot of chicks in a short time, since it might not eat again until the following year.

DID YOU KNOW?

Snakes that live their entire lives in salt water still need fresh water. They get it when it rains by drinking rainwater off the ocean's surface before it mixes with the sea's salt water.

IN SALT WATER

Sea snakes and kraits have flattened tails to help guide them through the water. Such snakes live in warm, tropical ocean waters and hunt fish and amphibians. So that they don't build up too much salt in their bodies from the water they live in, special glands in sea snakes' and kraits' mouths soak up excess salt. When the snakes flick their tongues to "smell," they flick out the extra salt.

FRESHWATER SWIMMERS

Lakes and rivers are home to snakes, too. In North America the cottonmouth is also known as the water moccasin because of its swimming ability. File snakes live in fresh water. Their pebbly skin helps them hold on to the wriggling fish that they hunt.

PRAIRIE RATTLESNAKE

Family: *Viperidae*
Species: *Crotalus viridis*

The prairie rattlesnake lives in desert and mountain areas throughout the American Southwest and Northwest. It has one of the widest ranges of any snake species in North America. The patterned skin of the prairie rattlesnake blends in with the snake's habitat.

Rattlesnakes are ambush predators, which means they lie in wait, camouflaged, until prey comes near. Then, like others in the viper family, they strike quickly, sinking their fangs in and injecting venom. After the venom has taken effect, paralyzing the victim, the snake then begins to eat. Rattlesnakes hunt rodents, birds, and lizards. They don't attack humans unless threatened by them, so the rattle is a great warning to back off.

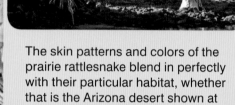

The skin patterns and colors of the prairie rattlesnake blend in perfectly with their particular habitat, whether that is the Arizona desert shown at right or the woodlands of Oregon.

SAD TRADITION

Some communities near rattlesnake habitats have annual rattlesnake roundups. Fearing that the snakes would attack them or their livestock, they began these roundups more than 50 years ago. People drive the snakes from their burrows using sticks, noise, dogs, or other tactics. They do this even though rattlesnakes only bite cows or horses when those animals step on them. When the snakes are cornered during the hunt, they are captured and killed. At some hunts, tens of thousands of snakes are caught and killed. Rattlesnake roundups are sometimes done by pouring gasoline into burrows. The smell of the gas drives out the snakes; the toxic fumes can even kill them outright. Conservationists are working hard to stop these activities.

The warning rattle of this snake is one of the scariest sounds in nature. Animals know that the sound signals that a venomous rattlesnake is nearby. The rattle is made of keratin, the same thing our fingernails are made of. When the snake vibrates its tail, the layers smack together, making the familiar rattling sound.

Vipers

The family of vipers is considered to be the most evolved snake family and includes some of the best-known snakes in the world. A key feature of vipers that distinguishes them from other snakes is the pair of hollow fangs that deliver venom directly into their prey with each strike.

STAR SNAKE

COMMON NAME
Prairie Rattlesnake

SCIENTIFIC NAME
Crotalus viridis

HABITAT
Desert, forest, grassland, mountain

LOCATIONS
Western and southwestern United States, northern Mexico, southwestern Canada

AVERAGE LENGTH
3 to 4 feet

FEEDS ON
Small mammals, birds, lizards

More than 30 species of rattlesnakes live in North and South America. Thanks to their noise-making tails, these vipers are one of the best-known types of snake. Though people may think of rattlesnakes as desert animals, they actually live in several different habitats.

Neotropical rattlesnakes live in the rainforests of South America and also the tropical islands of the Caribbean. They have a familiar diamond pattern on their skin and can be up to 6 feet long.

The pygmy rattlesnake is the smallest of the rattlers; most are less than 2 feet long. It lives in forest and woodland areas of America's southern states where rodent and small reptile prey is plentiful.

The Eastern diamondback is the largest rattlesnake. In fact, it's the biggest snake of any kind that lives in North America. It is up to 8 feet long and is found most often in Florida and some other Southern states.

The Mojave rattlesnake is a desert dweller, most commonly found near scrub brush in the open desert. Its powerful venom acts on prey's nerves, not the muscles and blood as with other rattlers.

RATTLESNAKES AND CULTURE

▶ Rattlesnake rattles are used as charms and as parts of jewelry.

▶ Some fiddlers and banjo players put rattles inside their instruments.

▶ Chippewa and Zuni Native American tribes include small family groups known as Rattlesnake Clans.

▶ Hopi tribes include rattlesnakes in their worship; the Hopi rattlesnake is named for the tribe.

FANG FACT

It's a myth that rattlesnakes get a new segment, or "button," on their rattle each year. Each time the snake sheds its skin, a new button is left on the rattle. But rattlesnakes shed their skin several times a year, so the number of rattles equals the number of sheddings, not years. However, the buttons are fragile and sometimes break off.

BANNER RATTLE

The timber rattlesnake is a part of American history. It has appeared on several flags, including one used by the original 13 colonies in the time of the American Revolution; on a U.S. Navy flag known as the Navy Jack; and on the state flag of New Hampshire. Benjamin Franklin described the timber rattlesnake as an emblem of magnanimity (generosity) and true courage.

American Vipers

Several viper species live in the United States, Canada, and Mexico. Like other vipers, they use their movable front fangs to bite and inject venom.

A DANGEROUS WIGGLE

Copperheads have a series of bold brown and orange bands, but the pattern stops at their light-brown or copper-colored head. These snakes live in thick woodlands. Young copperheads sometimes use the very thin tip of their tail as a lure to bring in prey. The slowly moving tip looks like a small worm and attracts frogs and other tasty treats for the snake to eat.

DOUG SAYS

Many of these viper species that were once quite abundant, such as the timber rattlesnake depicted on the first flag of the United States, are now critically endangered throughout much of their range.

—*Doug Hotle, Herpetologist*

Cottonmouth

WATER VIPER

The cottonmouth takes its common name from the inside of its mouth, which looks white like cotton. When threatened, it opens its mouth wide to warn off predators. This snake is up to 6 feet long and has a deadly bite. The cottonmouth is also known as the water moccasin. It spends most of its time in or near the water, living in lakes, ponds, and swamps in the American South.

Of the estimated 230 species of vipers, more than 150 are also known as pit vipers. They are named for their heat pits, the small organs located on the face. Like boas and pythons, which have numerous heat pits, pit vipers use these organs to find prey by sensing changes in temperature. This special sense also helps the snakes accurately aim a strike.

IRON HEAD

The fer-de-lance, a pit viper, gets its name from the shape of its head. The words in French mean "lance of iron." A lance is a type of spear with a triangle-shaped head, a shape similar to this snake's head. The fer-de-lance lives on the forest floor, camouflaged and lying in wait for prey. These snakes live in Central and South America.

Heat pit

MAKEUP

The eyelash pit viper has an interesting head feature. In addition to its heat pits, this snake has a pair of bristly, eyelashlike scales located above each eye. This colorful snake lives in trees in Central America.

Eyelash pit viper

DOUG SAYS

One of the most dangerous snakes on the planet is the Malayan pit viper. It bites many people each year, thanks to its habit of coiling, almost invisibly, on trails and well traveled pathways.

—*Doug Hotle, Herpetologist*

Some of the deadliest snakes in the world are vipers that live in Africa. Part of the reason is that snakes like the gaboon viper and the puff adder live in areas where there are many people, so there is a greater chance of snake–human encounters. These vipers are also good at camouflage, so they are hard for people to spot and avoid. Finally, medical help is often far away, and untreated bites can turn deadly.

SPOT THE SNAKE

Can you spot the gaboon viper at right? Its skin pattern blends in well among the leaves on a forest floor. The gaboon viper's triangular head even looks like a leaf. When prey comes by, the snake can strike with amazing speed. Check out the picture above to see what you're looking for.

Gaboon viper

REPTILE REPORT

When it isn't puffed up, the puff adder lies in wait to ambush prey. When a threat appears, it fills its neck and upper body with air to appear bigger. A predator might not attack this "bigger" adder.

ANOTHER RHINO?

The rhinoceros viper shares part of its name with the well-known African land mammal. While the rhino has a huge horn, the rhino viper has smaller horns that stick out from its snout. The horns are made of the same material as the scales that cover its body. The body scales of the rhinoceros viper form one of the most complex and colorful patterns seen on any snake.

This desert horned viper is named for its habitat—the desert—and for the two horns on its head. It burrows into the sand of its North African desert home. When it's done digging, only its eyes and the top of its head stick out from the sand. Two horns stick out, too. The horns are not for poking, however. Instead, they help keep the sand from filling the snake's eyes as it waits patiently for prey to wander by. Even when atop the sand, its coloring helps it blend in with the ground. Camouflage and surprise make the desert horned viper a successful predator.

HORNED SNAKES

Nearly all snakes have very smooth heads. However, some species sport horns or bumps. Here's a selection of the more unusual skull-toppers among snakes.

Gaboon Viper
This ambush predator lies in wait on the forest floor in African tropical regions.

Leaf-nosed Snake
The leaflike edge scales on this snake's nose help it hide in a tree.

FAMILY NEWS

There are more than 3,500 known snake species, and more are being discovered all the time. The viper family welcomed a new member in 2011. Matilda's horned viper, a colorful, 2-foot-long snake, was discovered in a forest in Tanzania. It was named by the scientist who discovered it; he named it for his daughter, Matilda.

Eyelash Pit Viper
The snake pictured here is yellow, but eyelash vipers can be red, brown, gray, or green, with many different skin patterns.

Many-horned Adder
This snake, which lives in southwestern Africa, can have from two to seven horns on its head.

Rhino Rat Snake
Scientists haven't yet discovered the reason for its nose spike, but it resembles that of a rhinoceros.

A dry and sandy desert might not seem like a great place to live, but for rattlesnakes and other vipers, it's ideal. They have all the features and abilities they need to survive in such harsh conditions.

HEAT SEEKERS

Like all reptiles, snakes are cold-blooded, which means they need to get their body warmth from the world around them. The hot desert environment makes this easy for snakes. They bask in the sun during the day. Under a rock ledge or curled into a sandy burrow, snakes soak up heat from the warm ground. The desert heat helps the snakes survive.

NIGHT MOVES

Desert snakes hunt at night. Snakes have numerous advantages when hunting in the dark. Extra-sharp senses, such as the ability to feel vibrations of other animals moving nearby and forked tongues that can "sniff" the air, allow them to seek out prey in the desert night.

DOUG SAYS

Many desert-dwelling snakes obtain the water they need from the prey they consume. The snake's body has adapted to lose very little moisture. A snake such as a sidewinder may go its entire life without a single drink of water.

—*Doug Hotle, Herpetologist*

The sidewinder is a type of rattlesnake. It lives in the deserts of the American Southwest. By moving sideways in coils, it ensures that only two or three areas of its body are on the hot sand at any time. Sidewinders are also recognized by the scaly "horns" over each eye, which may help keep the sand away from the eyes.

Revered and Feared

The *Viperidae* family includes many of the world's best-known and most feared snakes. They can be found in temples, are sometimes used in religious ceremonies, and the name often appears in popular culture.

SNAKES IN THE TEMPLE

Temple of the Azure Clouds in Penang, Malaysia, is also known as Snake Temple. For decades, numerous Wagler's pit vipers have made their home in the temple. The monks claim that the snakes do not bother them since they are in a sacred place. However, others suspect that the snakes are lulled by incense that is burned in the temple. Thousands of people visit, and the temple's monks claim no one has ever been bitten there by these deadly snakes.

REPTILE REPORT

The Wagler's pit viper (*Tropidolaemus wagleri*) is one of eight snakes or lizards named for herpetologist Johann Georg Wagler. He lived in Germany in the early 1800s, and helped to run a zoo in Munich.

MASTERFUL

The bushmaster is the largest member of the *Viperidae* family. A native of Central and South America, it can be up to 12 feet long. Its tail has a hard tip, which it shakes rapidly—and silently—when threatened. This scares off potential predators. Bushmasters are the only pit vipers in the Americas that lay eggs; these snakes sometimes protect their eggs, which is unusual behavior for snakes.

蛇

IN THE NEWS

The word "viper" represents power and force, and it has been used to name car models and airplanes. One of the characters in the movie *The Wolverine* is named Viper. And a serpentine character named Master Viper stars in the *Kung Fu Panda* movies.

The snake is one of 12 animals celebrated in the Chinese zodiac.

Like most reptiles, the majority of snakes lay eggs. The shells are not hard like bird eggs, however. They are softer and more flexible. Snake eggshells have been compared to thin leather or thick parchment. Not all snakes lay eggs; some species give birth to live babies.

Python hatchling breaking out of its soft egg

EGG-LAYERS

Snakes that lay eggs deposit the eggs in a group called a clutch. A clutch can be anywhere from 1 to 100 eggs, depending upon the species. The female snake chooses a site for a nest that can help protect the eggs, which many animals like to eat. The nest needs to be warm and moist, but not too wet, and hidden. Snakes might choose to lay eggs under logs, in small holes, or in burrows. Pythons, rat snakes, and cobras are some snakes that lay eggs.

Within each snake species, males and females mate to produce young. Snakes do not mate for life and may have several partners over time. Some snakes lay eggs that will later hatch, and others give birth to live babies.

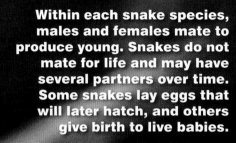

REPTILE REPORT

How does a baby snake break out of its egg? Snakes born inside eggs have a small hard scale at the tip of their snout called an egg tooth. They use this to slit the soft shell of the egg. Baby snakes lose this egg tooth the first time they shed their skin soon after they are born.

LIVE BIRTH

While some snakes lay eggs, others give birth to live babies, such as the hog-nosed pit viper shown here. Snakes born this way come out covered by a thin, gooey layer of tissue that they easily wriggle out of. As with snake babies from eggs, these young snakes have to fend for themselves right away. Snakes that give birth to live young include rattlesnakes, sea snakes, most vipers, and boas.

The Growing Years

Whether a snake comes out of an egg or is born live, it usually faces the world without help from its parents. At birth, a snake is ready to eat whatever its species normally eats. If it hunts and hides well, it has the best chance to survive. If not, it will be something else's meal.

Female African rock python brooding her clutch of eggs

DID YOU KNOW?

Snakes start growing as soon as they start eating after birth. And they never really stop growing for the rest of their lives. A snake is considered an adult when it is old enough to reproduce. Adulthood varies from species to species, ranging from less than a year to more than five for the largest species.

The female African rock python spends more time with its young than any other snake. It is known to coil itself around its eggs to protect them until they hatch. Called brooding, this is a rarity among snakes.

THE OTHER END OF LIFE

Every species is different, but some smaller snakes have shorter lives, from 2 or 3 to ten years, and larger snakes, such as pythons, live on average 20 to 30 years. The oldest snake on record is a male common boa named Popeye who lived at a Philadelphia Zoo. He was 40 years old when he died.

The Early Years

Snakes do not grow up in a family. Unlike humans and other mammals, nearly all snakes are self-sufficient when they are born. This means they are ready to find food and shelter and avoid enemies on their first day in the world. As a snake lives and grows, it prepares to play another important role—making more snakes.

BOY OR GIRL?

In most snake species, the physical differences between males and females are not obvious. Scientists say that snakes lack bold dimorphism, or gender differences. In general, female snakes have heavier bodies than males. Males often have longer tails. In some species, the males and females have slightly different head shapes or scales, but these are hard to spot for people who are not experts. Boomslang males can be green, and female boomslangs are always brown as shown here. This is visible evidence of dimorphism.

Newborn timber rattlesnakes will stay with their mother for about a week, until they first shed their skin. They have one "button" or rattle on their tail at birth.

GROWING GREENER

Most snakes look like their parents when they are born. Green tree pythons, however, look very different. When they are born, they are red, yellow, or orange. As they grow older, they slowly turn to an emerald green (at left). Scientists found that most younger tree pythons lived in a part of the rain forest where the bright color helped them blend in. As the snakes grow and change, they move to greener areas higher up in the forest canopy.

DOUG SAYS

A bite from a baby snake is *not* more or less deadly than one from an adult snake. The potency of the young snake and the adult snake venom is the same. People are often surprised that a baby snake, being so tiny, can deliver such a devastating bite. In any case, a bite from a deadly snake is bad news no matter how old the snake is.

—*Doug Hotle, Herpetologist*

SMALL-SCALED BURROWING ASP

Family: *Atractaspididae*
Species: *Atractaspis microlepidota*

It looks like a viper, but it's not. Like vipers, many of the species of burrowing asp have sharp fangs that can fold back. They're sometimes called stiletto snakes. (A stiletto is a type of thin-bladed knife.) But unlike a viper, which can only strike when its mouth is open, exposing the fangs, this asp can push its fangs outside the mouth and stab, injecting venom even when its mouth is closed.

This way of attacking prey works perfectly in the narrow underground burrows and tunnels where this asp looks for food. The asp swings its head side to side while hunting, fangs stabbing at small rodents it comes across. Since the burrows are often too narrow for the snake to even open its mouth, the side-stabbing fangs do the job. The venom for those fangs comes from a large gland. As much as 20 percent of a burrowing asp's body is taken up by this large gland.

Even experienced herpetologists need to take care when handling these snakes; they don't expect a snake to whip its head sideways and still be able to use its fangs. Venom from this snake can kill a person or at least make them very ill, and there is no antivenom for burrowing asp bites.

NOT MUCH ROOM TO EAT

Snakes do not chew their food—they swallow it whole. In the tight space of an underground tunnel, that can be tricky. When a burrowing asp eats, it expands as the prey is swallowed. But the snake is already squeezed into the tunnel. Also, it has no other teeth than its fangs. So how does it eat? The fangs hook the prey so the snake can pull it into the its mouth. Then the snake uses its jaws and neck muscles to squeeze or compress the prey and pull it into its body to digest. This ensures there is room for a full snake in a narrow tunnel.

REPTILE REPORT

Usually, a fanged snake lunges at its target from a short distance. This is called a strike. Burrowing asps are very close to their prey when they use their fangs (seen in close-up below), a move that is more of a stab than a strike.

Burrowing Asps

Unlike other burrowing species, the snakes in *Atractaspididae* sport sharp fangs but bites to humans are rare. The longest species in this family are 2 to 3 feet, and most are shaped like narrow tubes with no separation between neck and head.

STAR SNAKE

COMMON NAME
Small-scaled Burrowing Asp

SCIENTIFIC NAME
Atractaspis microlepidota

HABITAT
Underground burrow, forest floor

LOCATION
Central Africa

AVERAGE LENGTH
18 to 30 inches

FEEDS ON
Small rodents

Lizards Without Legs

For hundreds of millions of years, the largest reptiles ever were the dominant species on the earth. The mighty dinosaurs were reptiles, distant cousins of every snake, crocodile, and turtle in the world. Walking around underfoot in the time of the dinosaurs were early lizards, from which snakes evolved.

300 MILLION YEARS AGO

The first reptiles, called anapsids, first appeared. The oldest anapsid fossil discovered was of a small lizardlike creature called *Hylonomus*; it was about one foot long. Fifty million years later, reptiles were the dominant animals in the world. They had grown larger over time, and some had begun to look like small dinosaurs. Dinosaurs first appeared 240 million years ago. Walking on two legs, animals such as *Herrerasaurus* were as much as 13 feet tall.

150 MILLION YEARS AGO

By this time, dinosaurs had grown and evolved. Huge plant-eaters such as *Apatosaurus* emerged, along with mighty meat-eaters such as *Tyrannosaurus rex*. Many species of small lizards lived among the dinosaurs. Hunted by dinosaurs, some of the lizards began to live underground in order to survive. About 100 million years ago, snakelike creatures still had back legs, and over time more and more types of lizards became snakes.

65 MILLION YEARS AGO

Dinosaurs died out about 65 million years ago, while some smaller reptiles, including snakes, survived this mass extinction. The variety of snakes began to expand rapidly 30 million years ago. Early boas, vipers, and snakes similar to cobras were growing in number.

The thousands of snake species in the world today evolved over millions of years from lizards, which have been around even longer. In that time, each species of snake has evolved to best survive in its own habitat.

DOUG SAYS

For a long time, paleontologists focused on dinosaurs. Now, we are looking at reptile evolution as never before. We are still learning more about how reptiles evolved.

—*Doug Hotle,*
Herpetologist

World's Biggest Snake

Paleontologists are scientists who study fossils for clues as to what animals looked like long ago and how they evolved to become the animals we see today. Fossils and fossil impressions found in rocks, known collectively as fossil records, teach us many things about the natural world. Fossil records of reptiles show the stages of evolution that, step by step, changed some types of lizards into snakes. They also show how closely many of today's reptiles resemble their ancient ancestors.

BIGGEST SNAKE EVER

In 2009, a report about the discovery of the biggest snake ever made headlines around the world. After careful study, it was announced that the fossil bones of the world's largest snake had been found. A skull was found in 2011 that confirmed the finding. Named Titanoboa, the snake lived more than 55 million years ago in a South American swamp. It lived during the time of the dinosaurs, and survived after dinosaurs became extinct. This super snake was nearly 50 feet long and weighed about 2,500 pounds, making it as big as a school bus. It is the longest snake ever found.

SMART METHOD

The small bone is from a modern-day anaconda, the heaviest snake species alive today. The larger bone is from the gigantic Titanoboa. By comparing these, scientists were able to estimate Titanoboa's length and weight.

FANG FACT

One theory about Titanoboa's size has to do with the climate. In those long-ago days, the average temperature in South America was much higher than it is now. Since snakes use energy to regulate their body temperature from the outside air, a hotter climate meant a snake could have a greater ability to grow much bigger. With so much heat to take in year-round, this giant snake flourished.

A full-scale replica of the prehistoric snake Titanoboa, at Grand Central Terminal in New York City, promoted the "Titanoboa: Monster Snake" exhibit at the Smithsonian's National Museum of Natural History in Washington, DC. The man standing nearby gives an idea of the massive scale of this early snake.

COMMON GARTER SNAKE

Family: *Colubridae*
Species: *Thamnophis sirtalis*

If you've come across a snake in the wild in North America, it was probably a garter snake. The common garter snake has at least eight subspecies, making it among the most prevalent snakes on the continent. These snakes are easy to identify thanks to the long stripe that runs along their entire body. However, they come in a wide variety of colors and patterns to go with that stripe. In some parts of the United States, garter snakes are entirely black. They have a wide range of lengths, too, from 18 to 45 inches and sometimes longer.

Garter snakes often live near water and can be spotted near ponds and lakes. They are also popular pets. Like all snakes, they bite, but they don't have fangs and their teeth are located very far back in their mouths so they aren't dangerous to people.

Within a few hours of birth, garter snakes are independent. They are born live, not in eggs, and have to quickly find their own food.

Garter snakes hibernate during colder months, typically in large groups. In warm weather, they are active and can often be found basking in the sun to keep their temperature up.

DEFENSE AND OFFENSE

Because they live over such a wide area, garter snakes are hunted by many other animals, from raccoons to snapping turtles to herons. When grabbed, a garter snake whips around its thin body furiously, trying to escape. It releases a very stinky fluid that might chase off an attacker. The signature stripe down the back of many garter snakes helps it hide in the grass.

DID YOU KNOW?

This snake gets part of its common name from the stripe up its back, which resembles a piece of clothing that was once commonly worn by men. A garter is a stretchy cloth worn around the leg to hold up a sock.

Colubrids

The largest family of snakes—with more than 2,000 species—Colubrids are found on every continent except Antarctica. They are united in a family mostly for their basic shape and because they don't really fit into any other, smaller family.

STAR SNAKE

COMMON NAME

Common Garter Snake

SCIENTIFIC NAME

Thamnophis sirtalis

HABITAT

Meadow, forest floor, freshwater edge, and other moist, grassy areas

LOCATION

Most of North America

AVERAGE LENGTH

18 to 45 inches

FEEDS ON

A wide variety of small animals, including snakes, frogs, birds, snails, slugs, and more.

Garter snakes coming out of hibernation

Colubrids are found on every continent except Antarctica, and with more than about 2,000 species worldwide, *Colubridae* is the largest snake family. The United States is home to several hundred Colubrid (koh-LOO-brid) species.

MILK SHAKE? NO, MILK *SNAKE*.

Milk snakes create a lot of confusion. First, most species of milk snakes have scales with bands of red, yellow, and black. They look similar to the dangerous coral snake, but milk snakes are harmless to humans. Second, their name is a mistake. These snakes were often seen near farms and barns and people came to think that they sucked milk from cows. They do not, but the name stuck.

FANG FACT

Colubrids come in hundreds of shapes and colors. One trait they share is that none of them has a working left lung; they use only their right lung to breathe. In some Colubrids, the left lung is absent and they have only one lung.

RAT SNAKES

Five different types of rat snake live in the American South and Texas. (There are also rat snakes that live in Asia and South America.) The species in the U.S. can be as long as 6 feet, and they come in a wide variety of colors and patterns. Rat snakes live in nearly every habitat in the U.S., including forests, ponds, deserts, and grasslands. As the name suggests, rodents are their main prey.

DOUG SAYS

Scientists first classified snakes based solely on how they looked. That meant that over half of the snake species were dumped into the Colubrid family. However, modern science techniques, such as looking at DNA, can now help us better sort this "junk drawer" of snake species.

—*Doug Hotle, Herpetologist*

HAIL TO THE KING

Ten different kinds of kingsnakes live in North America. Along with garter snakes, they are among the most common snakes in the U.S. Kingsnakes live everywhere from Florida to Texas to California, and as far south as Mexico. While they will eat almost any animal they come across, kingsnakes can, and often do, eat other snakes. They are immune to the venom of rattlesnakes and copperheads.

Kingsnake eating a rattlesnake

Colorful and easy to handle and care for, corn snakes are among the most popular snakes to keep as pets. They can be found in tanks and terrariums in classrooms and in people's homes. In the wild, they live mostly in the southern U.S., Texas, and northern Mexico.

FANG FACT

Many think the corn snake's name comes from early American settlers. They found the snakes in their cornfields and cribs (places where harvested corn was stored). The snakes were not eating the corn; they were feeding on the rodents that lived in the field and cribs.

SNAKES AS PETS

Like any pet, snakes have special needs. Snake owners must give pet snakes a comfortable, safe place to live. A tank should be big enough for the snake species that will live in it. All snakes need to have water in a tray or bowl. The bottom of the tank should be covered with material proper for the snake. The material should be changed or cleaned often. Owners should know what to feed their snakes. With proper care, corn snakes can be excellent pets.

DOUG SAYS

Although a pet snake requires less time than a dog or cat, a snake is still a big responsibility for any pet owner. Study as much as you can *before* getting your new pet. Be prepared to provide the best care and attention that you can.

—*Doug Hotle, Herpetologist*

COLORFUL CORN SNAKES

Corn snakes come in different colors and patterns, and some people who breed the snakes create many new types, or "morphs." The large snake pictured pictured is a wild corn snake; the small circle pictures show morphs, created by mixing genetic information through breeding.

The family of Colubrid snakes has the widest range of any of the snake families. There are Colubrids in just about every country in the world. The wide variety of species and locations means they have found homes in dozens of habitats.

LOOK! UP IN THE AIR!

A flying snake? The paradise tree snake living in Southeast Asia can glide from tree to tree in the rainforest. This snake is able to spread its ribs to glide on updrafts (air rising from the ground). It's not really flying, but by flattening its body it can glide with control and direction.

A WORLD OF COLUBRIDS

From desert to ocean, from forest to field, Colubrids have adapted to different living situations around the world.

Desert: Banded sand snakes skim easily over the soft desert sands; they also burrow into the sand to catch insects.

Houses: The aurora house snake may be found in South African homes, where it tracks down rodents and keeps houses pest-free.

ANOTHER FLYER

Along with the flying snake and some lizard species, some squirrels can glide from branch to branch. Large skin flaps extend to catch the air.

Water: Water snakes, such as this brown-banded water snake, spend most of their time swimming in freshwater, looking for prey.

Grasslands: The indigo snake is more than 8 feet long. It lives in grassy areas and on forest floors.

Rainforest: The mangrove snake finds a plentiful food supply in the steamy rainforests of Southeast Asia.

Super Skinny

Snakes in general are long and thin. This size and shape is one of the things that make them snakes. But some snakes, including several members of the *Colubridae* family, are especially skinny.

FANG FACT

Some racers move through tall grass with their heads elevated above the grass like a periscope. This helps them spot movement that could be prey.

THIN AND FAST

The names of some of the thinnest Colubrids tell their tale. The red-tailed racer can move very quickly over flat ground. Black racers move fast and eat fast, too. They don't constrict or bite; they just eat whatever they catch whole—and alive. Whip snakes and coachwhips do, as their names suggest, look like whips, and are quick as whips, too. With their speed, they can catch many of the lizards and small amphibians that they chase.

Coachwhip snake

IN THE TREES

Being very slender and lightweight is a big advantage for Colubrids that live in trees. Green vine snakes, for example, can balance on a branch that would not support a larger snake. They also hide among those branches and leaves. The blunthead tree snake has an extremely thin body. This helps it move easily among even small and thin branches. When a vine snake homes in on prey, it moves very slowly and even sways back and forth like a twig in the breeze.

Green vine snake

DID YOU KNOW?

The Malagasy leaf-nosed snake (shown here) has a series of scales and ridges on the end of its snout.

This blunthead tree snake, which can grow to about 3 feet long, is slender and light enough to crawl across the thin leaves of a palm tree. It lives in Central and South America.

Only a few—perhaps only a half dozen—of the approximately 2,000 Colubrids are dangerous to humans. Colubrids have fangs at the back of their upper jaw and are known as rear-fanged. This feature makes it less likely that they will bite a person. With some exceptions, they also have weak venom designed to kill small animals.

KNIFE SKILLS

Kukri snakes take their name from the way their sharp, curved rear fangs resemble a knife used by Gurkha soldiers. Kukri snakes use these sharp fangs to slice through the shells of bird and reptile eggs they eat. While kukris are not known to bite humans, they may if provoked, slicing rather than puncturing the skin with their fangs.

WHAT'S FOR DINNER?

Some Colubrid species are named for the foods they eat, including these snakes. Here is a look at the prey they seek.

Common Rhombic Egg-eater
Lives in Africa, and seeks bird and reptile eggs.

Mole Snake
Native to much of southern Africa; lives mostly underground, and eats moles.

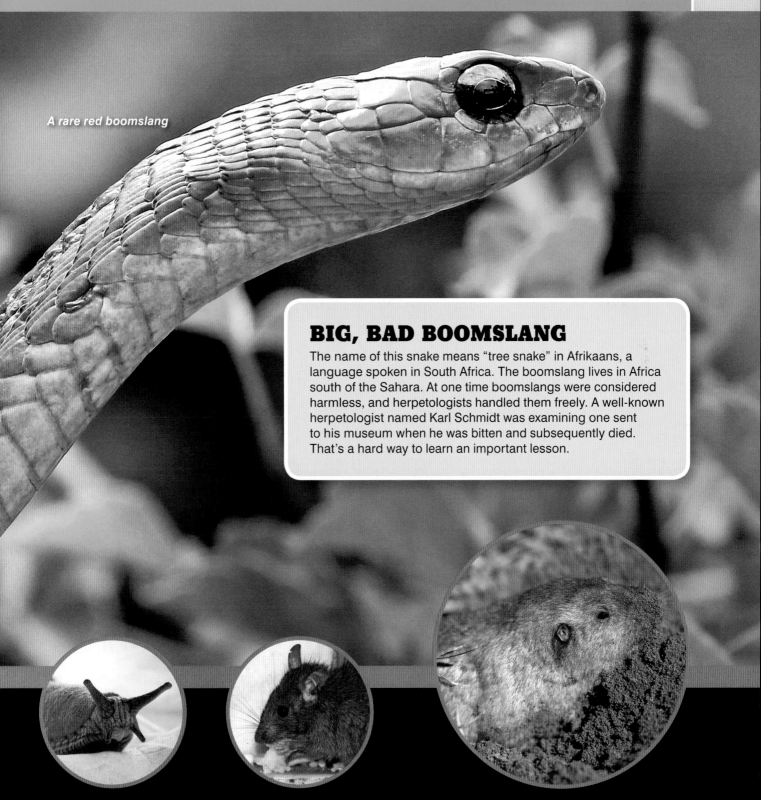

A rare red boomslang

BIG, BAD BOOMSLANG

The name of this snake means "tree snake" in Afrikaans, a language spoken in South Africa. The boomslang lives in Africa south of the Sahara. At one time boomslangs were considered harmless, and herpetologists handled them freely. A well-known herpetologist named Karl Schmidt was examining one sent to his museum when he was bitten and subsequently died. That's a hard way to learn an important lesson.

Slug- and Snail-eater
Found in Central and South America; their lower jaw can push out to pull snails

Rat Snake
A constrictor that eats rodents and birds, including its namesake—rats.

Gopher Snake
A common snake native to North America; eats small mammals, including gophers.

A Colorful Family

Scientists group *Colubridae* together for their general body shape—slim and straight—and for shared internal features that include some spine and skull bones and a nonworking left lung. Within the family, however, Colubrids show off a wide range of colors and decorations. They come in almost every color of the rainbow, so it's hard to pick one that is the most colorful, but here are some contenders.

Asian vine snakes look for lizards to eat among the leaves and branches of the moist rainforests in Sri Lanka and much of Southeast Asia.

A coral snake mimic, the yellow-headed calico snake hunts during the day, searching for rodents, lizards, and frogs.

Usually 4 to 6 feet long, trinket snakes live in Southeast Asia and prey on lizards and small amphibians.

This pygmy snake is the smallest of the African wolf snake species, at only about a foot long.

The striped bamboo rat snake lives in several regions of Asia where it thrives in temperate rainforest and mountainous habitats.

The San Francisco garter snake is considered by many to be the most beautiful snake in North America, with its body-long multicolored stripes.

RAREST OF ALL?

Once thought to be extinct, recent discoveries of the St. Lucia racer on a small island in the Caribbean have upgraded its status. It is now considered one of the rarest in the world. There may be fewer than 100 of the forest-dwelling, 3-foot-long snakes left. Efforts are under way to help save this species.

San Francisco garter snake

Extreme Snakes

Measuring snakes is pretty tricky. Live snakes expand and contract their bodies to move. And most species of snake continue to grow throughout their lives.

REPTILE REPORT

The most-asked question about snakes is: What's the biggest snake? There are two answers to this. One measurement that scientists use is length; the other is weight. In the world of snakes, the longest snake is not the heaviest, so there are two "biggest" snakes.

HEAVIEST SNAKE

A member of the *Boidae* family, the green anaconda weighs in at more than 250 pounds. One specimen tipped the scales at 550 pounds.

SHORT SNAKE

Curled up, a thread snake from the Caribbean island of Barbados fits on a quarter. Moving in a straight line, it's only about 4 inches long. The thread snake lays only one egg a year—and it's a pretty tiny egg.

LONGEST SNAKE

Exact measurements of snakes are hard to make; just holding them still to measure is a real challenge. However, the reticulated python, at about 25 feet long, is regarded as the longest species of snake.

With more than 3,500 species to choose from, some snakes stand out as the longest, heaviest, shortest . . . and longest-lived.

LONGEST FANGS

The gaboon viper has fangs that are about 2 inches long, the biggest of any fanged snake.

LIFE CYCLE RECORDS

MOST BABIES AT ONE TIME

Snakes lay eggs or give birth to live young. Snake mothers will usually have from 1 to 100 babies, depending on the species. Puff adders give birth to live young and give birth to the most babies at one time. The most ever recorded by a puff adder in captivity was 156.

MOST BABIES IN A LIFETIME

The puff adder is certainly in the running for having the most babies in a lifetime. But the African house snake might hold the title for most babies. This fertile snake gives birth to clutches of 5 to 10 eggs at a time, and it gives birth 7 to 8 times each year. If it lived to be 20 years old, that would be more than 1,500 eggs.

LONGEST-LIVED SPECIES

There is no exact way of knowing how long some rare species of snake live, but larger snakes tend to live longer lives. A ball python survived for 47 years at a Philadelphia Zoo and died in 1991. Since it was a few years old when it arrived, it might have been older than 50.

Deadly Deeds

One snake record really seems to intrigue people: What is the deadliest snake in the world? There is actually a lot of debate about that. Luckily, scientists love a good debate. As you'll see, there are many ways snakes can be deadly.

DEADLIEST SEA SNAKE

The banded sea snake's venom is the most lethal, but the beaked sea snake causes more deaths. It is more aggressive and often gets tangled in fishing nets, sometimes with deadly results for a boat crew member.

DEADLIEST LAND SNAKE

The inland taipan is considered the most venomous land snake. Its venom could kill a person less than 20 minutes after a bite.

FASTEST MOVER

The black mamba is not only one of the most venomous snakes in the world, it is also the fastest. It can speed along the ground at up to 14 miles per hour. So it's best not to annoy a black mamba.

DEADLIEST CONSTRICTOR

Any large constricting snake—boa, python, and anaconda—can make short work of killing just about any small animal. The green anaconda—the largest snake in the world—is also the strongest. It can kill the largest animals known among snake prey.

THE MOST SNAKE-FILLED PLACE IN THE WORLD

While there are snakes all over the world, there is one place where there are so many deadly snakes that no people can visit. Located off the coast of Brazil, Ilha de Queimada Grande is only one-tenth as big as New York's Central Park. But it is so covered with golden lancehead snakes that the Brazilian government forbids anyone from going there! The snakes have no predators on the island and find plenty to eat among visiting birds. The golden lancehead's venom is particularly strong, and can kill a person very quickly.

COUNTRY WITH THE MOST SNAKEBITES

India has the greatest number of deaths from snake bite, at nearly 50,000 people a year. A mix of a crowded population and a climate that is perfect for tropical snakes—including cobras and vipers—means snakes and people often come in contact. Many of the deaths are in rural areas where medical treatment is far away. In Australia, home to many more venomous snakes, fatal bites are relatively rare, averaging one or two a year.

COUNTRY WITH THE MOST DEADLY SNAKES

Australia is home to at least a dozen of the snakes most dangerous to humans. However, the snakes often live in remote areas, so deaths from snakebite are rare even in this land of venomous serpents.

COUNTRY WITH THE FEWEST SNAKES

Antarctica isn't a country, it is a continent, and no snakes live there. Ireland is famous for having no snakes, and legend says that Saint Patrick chased them out more than a thousand years ago. The actual reason is that melting glaciers and rising seas cut Ireland off from the rest of Europe about 10,000 years ago, before snakes had a chance to populate it. Other island nations without snakes include New Zealand and Iceland.

KING COBRA

Family: *Elapidae*
Species: *Ophiophagus hannah*

King cobras live in heavily forested areas from China to India, as well as in the Philippines. Their venom is highly toxic; a bite from a large cobra can kill an elephant. They are also the longest venomous snakes in the world—some as long as 19 feet have been found. What is the king cobra's main diet? Other snakes, including venomous types. Its scientific name is derived from a Greek word meaning snake-eating snake.

The king cobra, like most snakes, tends to avoid confrontation, but when it is challenged it has a number of defensive warnings, also called threat displays. The king cobra can spread its hood to make it look larger and more intimidating; it makes a sound called a hissing growl described as a loud, low grumble; and it can raise its head high above the ground. Still moving forward in this raised position, the king cobra can strike and bite as far as 10 feet away from its body.

SCARE TACTIC

The distinctive king cobra neck hood has flexible ribs. Eight muscles move to rotate the ribs outward. It makes the snake look bigger and warns off predators. The king cobra has a strike and bite range of as much as 10 feet.

Elapids

Elapids might be part of *Colubridae* if not for the fixed fangs that these snakes possess. Elapids live in many different environments and habitats. This family includes cobras, kraits, mambas, and other well-known—and dangerous—snake species.

STAR SNAKE

COMMON NAME
King Cobra

SCIENTIFIC NAME
Ophiophagus hannah

HABITAT
Forest

LOCATIONS
Southern India, Southeast Asia, Indonesia

AVERAGE LENGTH
12 to 16 feet

FEEDS ON
Snakes, rodents, lizards

FANG FACT

King cobras are the only known snake to build a nest for their eggs. The female cobra gathers up leaves and other vegetation to cover the eggs. She then curls her body around them for protection. The male stays nearby to guard.

More Than Just the King

Cobras are the best-known members of the *Elapidae* family. In fact, they're among the most recognizable snakes in the world. The king cobra often gets the most attention, but this group of snakes is much more than just royalty.

A REAL CHARMER

In India, street performers play the flute while a cobra seems to dance, hypnotized, out of a basket in front of the player. Called snake charming, it is actually a kind of trick. The snake's attention is not on the music, but rather on the movement of the flute. The snake charmer knows to sit far enough away that if the cobra strikes, it won't reach the charmer.

REPTILE REPORT

The monocled cobra, often used in snake charming, has a single mark on the back of its hood. (A monocle is an eyeglass worn on just one eye.) An Indian legend says that Buddha kissed the snake there long ago after it helped provide shade while Buddha slept.

DID YOU KNOW?

What can defeat a king cobra? As powerful as cobras are, they meet their match in a small mammal called a mongoose. These animals have evolved to have speed and an ability to withstand cobra bites.

SPITTING IMAGE

The spitting cobra does just what its name says—it spits venom when attacked, aiming at an attacker's eyes. While the predator is blinded (usually temporarily), the snake escapes. Spitting cobras can shoot their venom 8 to 10 feet. The venom shoots out from holes in the front of the snake's fangs. This is a defense mechanism for the snake, not a way to catch prey. If the venom fails to stop the predator, a spitting cobra will, and frequently does, bite.

Copycats

Worth, Central, and South America are home to more than 60 species of coral snake. What sets the many types of coral snakes apart from one another is that their multiple bands of color vary. Because coral snakes are quite venomous, they have many copycats in nature. Other snakes evolved to look like corals to get this "scary" protection.

COOL SCIENCE TERM

The name for this evolution-based animal copying is called "Batesian mimicry" after an English explorer named Henry Walter Bates.

BEE VS. FLY

For an example of Batesian mimicry in nature, check out this honeybee and this syrphid fly. Can you tell which is which? The fly hopes its predators can't tell.

Top photo is the honeybee; bottom photo is the syrphid fly.

MENACE OR MIMIC?

Can you pick out the snakes that are menaces and those that are mimics? Some nonvenomous snakes have evolved with coloration that mimics, or looks like, that of the venomous coral snake. This feature helps the mimicking snakes warn off predators, who may think they have encountered a menace—a deadly coral snake—and back off.

Experts say to keep this rhyme in mind when looking at snakes in the U.S.: Red and black, okay for Jack; Red and yellow, kill a fellow.

Top row, left to right: eastern coral snake; nonvenomous kingsnake; nonvenomous Western shovelnose snake
Bottom row, left to right: Peruvian coral snake; Allen's coral snake; nonvenomous Arizona mountain kingsnake

Kraits in the Night

The Elapids known as kraits are snakes that people should avoid. However, as kraits' habitats often include towns and villages in India and Southeast Asia, this is not always easy. During the day, these shy snakes are very hard to find. But when night falls, they become deadly hunters. The good news for humans is that kraits most often hunt other snakes.

REPTILE REPORT

Some kraits spend most of their time in the sea. The banded sea krait has a two-headed defense strategy. Its tail looks like its head, so attackers can be fooled into aiming at the wrong end.

The eyes of a krait have very large, round pupils, which help the snake see better at night.

Banded sea kraits can live in the water or on land. They often swim to shore and slither onto the land, where they can be seen basking on the rocks and sand. They also mate, shed their skin, and find fresh water to drink when on land.

Sea krait

KRAIT VS. COBRA

Both kraits and cobras are part of the *Elapidae* family, but they don't act like family. Kraits are often eaten by cobras, which are not harmed by kraits' normally deadly venom.

While most snakes are round or cylindrical (tubelike) in shape, banded kraits have compressed sides and look almost triangular. Their spine is raised more than is typical in a snake's body.

While elapids and vipers are very similar, they evolved as separate snake families in most parts of the world. However, on the isolated continent of Australia, where dozens of species of the *Elapidae* family live, the elapids stayed as a single family. The death adder and tiger snake look quite viperlike, but they are true elapids.

WORLD'S DEADLIEST SNAKE?

It goes by many names—fierce snake, small-scaled snake, inland taipan—but to experts it is known as the world's most lethal land snake. The venom from a single bite is said to be powerful enough to kill 250,000 mice. The inland taipan doesn't often bite people; it is reclusive and lives far from most humans in the desert habitat of the Australian Outback. While a bite from an inland taipan could kill a person in less than an hour, all known bites have been successfully treated with antivenom. Its cousin, the coastal taipan, is more aggressive, nearly as lethal, and is responsible for deadly snake-human encounters.

DOUG SAYS

Why are there no vipers in Australia? The vipers separated from the elapids after the great land mass Pangaea broke apart hundreds of millions of years ago. Living in isolation on Australia, elapids did not evolve into true vipers as they did in other places. The Australian elapids do look a lot like vipers, however.

—*Doug Hotle, Herpetologist*

SNAKE VS. TOAD

Australia's common death adder (above) is stuck with a misleading name. It is not common at all and its numbers are going down. It can kill humans but rarely does. And it's not really an adder: Adders are vipers and there are no vipers in Australia. It got the name a long time ago because it resembled an adder, and the name has not changed. Death adders have another problem—the cane toad. This large, poisonous amphibian was introduced into Australia in 1935 and has proliferated. Death adders can die from eating this type of toad. Up against both the cane toad and human population growth that is reducing their habitat, death adders are in trouble.

The black mamba is one of the most feared and deadly snakes in the world. It lives only in southern and eastern Africa, and it is considered Africa's deadliest snake. Its powerful venom can kill a person in 20 minutes if help does not arrive. At up to 13 feet long, the black mamba is also the longest venomous snake in Africa.

MAMBA LEGENDS

In southeast Africa, the black mamba has a fearsome reputation. Over the years, stories and legends have grown up around it.

▶ **Black mambas can strike the length of their body:** Not true. They can reach only about a third of their body length to hit a target.

▶ **Black mambas can kill an elephant:** This actually might be true. There are documented stories of elephants dying after mamba strikes. However, the physical condition of the elephants before the snake strikes is not known.

▶ **Black mambas can stand on the tip of their tail:** Not true, despite what some legends say.

▶ **Black mambas will chase a person down in order to attack:** Not exactly true. The snake will advance if it perceives a threat. If the person turns and runs away (highly recommended!), the snake will end the offensive.

UP IN THE TREES

Three species of green mamba spend most of their life in the trees on the southeast coast of Africa. They eat mostly birds and bats. Hidden by camouflage, they strike at moving animals or sneak up on resting ones. While the East African green mamba has the least potent venom of the mamba species, the venom is powerful enough to be deadly.

WHY "BLACK" MAMBA?

The black mamba is not black. Its scales are mostly gray or silver in various patterns. Its name comes from the inside of its mouth. When threatened, the black mamba opens its mouth wide, revealing that the inside is a dark black color.

DID YOU KNOW?

The great NBA star Kobe Bryant of the Los Angeles Lakers is nicknamed The Black Mamba. Why? This snake is fast and can strike accurately and repeatedly—which is the way Kobe Bryant plays basketball.

SPECIAL SKILLS

The black mamba can spread the skin around its head into a cobralike hood to appear larger to an attacker. If the black mamba attacks, it is famous for biting several times quickly instead of in just a single strike like most vipers. The black mamba is also the fastest snake in the world, able to move as fast as a sprinting person for short distances.

Some snakes are indeed dangerous, but people tend to fear *all* snakes. In fact, most are not dangerous to people. The ones that are live in specific areas and can be avoided. When good medical care is available, the chances of dying from a venomous snake's bite are very small.

DOUG SAYS

The number-one thing to remember if you see a snake in the wild: Never, ever threaten the snake by trying to capture or kill it. Chances are that this will result in you being bitten. If you see a snake, leave it alone! Walk around it or in the other direction. Take a picture from a safe distance, but otherwise don't bother the snake…and it won't bother you.

—*Doug Hotle, Herpetologist*

WORD!

Ophidiophobia (oh-FIH-dee-oh-FOH-bee-ah) means "fear of snakes." "Ophis" is Greek for "snake," while "phobia" means "fear."

FACT OR MYTH?

There are many myths about snakes, and they come from misunderstanding snake behavior or from folk tales handed down over time.

Can you guess which of these are myths?

➡ Snakes drink milk.
➡ Snakes can bite their tails and roll like a hoop.
➡ Snakes have poisonous breath.
➡ Snakes hypnotize their prey by staring.
➡ Snakes always travel in pairs.
➡ Snakes chase people.

These are all myth. Snakes drink only water. They travel in pairs only when mating or coming out of hibernation (snakes may hibernate in groups). If they are startled, they might take off in the same direction as you or you might simply be in the way of their favorite hiding place, but snakes don't chase people.

SMOOTH OPERATORS

Snakes are not slimy. That is one myth about snakes that increases the fear of them. Snakes are actually dry to the touch, smooth, and not wet at all. Perhaps people think snakes feel slimy because worms, frogs, and salamanders sometimes do. Those last two are amphibians, but people can confuse the two animal orders.

An extreme fear of snakes—ophidiophobia—is one of the most common phobias, or unfounded fears. Snakes are an important part of just about every ecosystem on the planet. (An ecosystem is a community of living organisms like animals and plants, and their habitats.) Many people's fears might be eased by knowledge of the facts.

WORSE THAN SNAKES

According to the University of Florida, here is a comparison of some of the ways people in the United States die each year.

54 LIGHTNING STRIKE DEATHS

53 BEE OR WASP STING DEATHS

21 DOG BITE DEATHS

6 SNAKEBITE DEATHS

Green pit viper

Rogues' Gallery

While the vast majority of snakes don't harm humans, some can and do. Here are some of the most dangerous snakes in the world.

RATTLESNAKE

The rattlesnake is one of the few snakes found in the United States that is considered among the world's most dangerous. Common in the Southeast and desert Southwest of the United States, they can strike more than half the length of their body when threatened.

COASTAL TAIPAN

The venom from this Australian snake, the coastal taipan, is highly toxic and can result in a quick death. The inland taipan's venom is more lethal, but the snake rarely encounters humans.

VIPER

This saw-scaled viper's bite isn't the most venomous, but it results in more deaths than any other snake in the world because it lives so close to people and many bites occur.

PUFF ADDER

The puff adder is not an aggressive snake, and it relies on camouflage for protection. It lives close to populated areas in parts of Africa and the southern part of the Arabian Peninsula, and is often inadvertently stepped on, resulting in numerous bites on humans.

THE GOOD NEWS In many areas of the world, medicine called antivenom is available to help snakebite victims. The antivenom is made from venom itself. The faster the antivenom can be given to victims, the better their odds of surviving. Experts say that anyone bitten by a snake of any kind should seek medical attention.

BANDED SEA KRAIT

The venom of banded sea kraits is ten times as toxic as that of rattlesnakes, but they are considered shy and rarely encounter people. Banded sea kraits are amphibious, meaning they can live in water and on land; however, they spend most of their time in the water.

BLACK MAMBA

The black mamba can stab repeatedly with its fangs, delivering high doses of fast-acting venom. Considered aggressive, these snakes can move at more than 14 miles an hour.

CORAL SNAKE

Coral snakes have highly toxic venom, but cause few bites and deaths. They live in close proximity to people, who often encounter them. However, they rarely bite people due to their placid demeanor.

CAPE COBRA

The Cape cobra is the most dangerous of all African cobras. Only about 4 feet long, the Cape cobra is a highly aggressive and nervous snake. Its bite can be fatal within 30 minutes, and more than half of all bites result in death.

Other Reptiles

Lizards can move with lightning speed. Turtles and tortoises plod along. Crocodiles fiercely attack their prey. Tuataras, whose ancient relatives lived alongside dinosaurs, are considered "living fossils." All these animals are different in many ways, but they also share traits, and along with snakes comprise the group of animals known as reptiles.

A common iguana, known as an Iguana iguana, displaying its colors

PANTHER CHAMELEON

Family: *Chamaeleonidae*
Species: *Furcifer pardalis*

Chameleons are perhaps the best known among the nearly 6,000 species of lizards. In an animal world of green, brown, and gray, these colorful creatures really stand out. They come in a range of colors, and some can even change color. The panther chameleon, which is normally olive green, has a huge range of colors. It can turn parts of its skin orange, green, pink, purple, or red. There are many reasons to make a color change. Often the purpose of a color change is to attract a mate; or to challenge rivals; or to hide better in a treetop home by matching nature's colors.

Panther chameleons live in the northern part of the island of Madagascar, off Africa's southeast coast. Different groups of panther chameleons can have different color patterns, which can vary from one part of the forest to another.

Like most lizards, chameleons eat insects as their main food. They shoot out a long, sticky tongue to snatch insects from trees or from the air. Chameleons move very slowly and can stay still for hours. They wait for insects to come near and then *zap*—they eat.

A chameleon can shoot out its tongue more than one and a half times its body length to snare prey.

Lizards

Few types of animals come in as many colors and varieties as lizards. From tiny geckos to massive monitor lizards, there are nearly 6,000 lizard species living in various habitats around the world.

STAR LIZARD

COMMON NAME
Panther Chameleon

SCIENTIFIC NAME
Furcifer pardalis

HABITAT
Trees, forests

LOCATION
Madagascar

AVERAGE LENGTH
1 to 2 feet

FEEDS ON
Insects

AMAZING EYES

When a person looks at something, the eyes point in one direction. A chameleon, however, can have its eyes pointing in different directions. The eyes can move in a full circle, and can watch two things at once. This helps in watching for predators as well as searching for fast-moving insect prey.

Four legs, a tail, scaly skin, eyelids—nearly every lizard shares these features. But the lizard order is more than a collection of similar body parts. Lizards have unique features that set them apart from their reptile cousins.

WHAT MAKES A LIZARD A LIZARD?

▶ Most lizards have excellent eyesight, and many species can see in full color.

▶ Most lizards have eyelids, which is one major difference from snakes.

▶ Lizards have ears; they are openings in the skin without flaps.

▶ Lizards have flexible fingers, which are good for grabbing branches.

Lizardlike *Seymouria* lived about 270 million years ago. It was only 2 feet long. *Seymouria* is a link in the evolutionary chain from prehistoric reptiles to today's lizards.

A TALE OF TAILS

Some lizards have a unique form of self-defense; they can lose part of their tail to a predator and regrow it later. In fact, some species can make it fall off through a process called caudal autonomy. Skinks are well known for this behavior. A predator will chase the still-wiggling tail end while the lizard escapes.

Tail

Tongue

Eyelid

Eye

Nostril

Ear opening

Claws

DINNER TIME

Many lizards are carnivores; the vast majority eat only insects. The enormous monitor lizard eats meat from numerous types of animals. Iguanas and similar lizards, including the Calotes lizard shown on the right, eat insects as well as plants.

Lizards live on every continent in the world except Antarctica. They have adapted to just about every kind of habitat, from wet rainforests to dry deserts, from soggy marshlands to temperate forests.

LOVING THE WATER

Marine iguanas on the Galápagos Islands spend more of their lives in the water than any other lizard. They have long claws that help them hold onto underwater rocks while they feed on kelp. Their tails act as rudders for steering while swimming. They have to breathe air, but can stay underwater for several minutes at a time.

GETTING A LITTLE SUN

As cold-blooded reptiles, lizards need to get body warmth from the environment. They will often be seen resting in the sun, building up body heat lost during cool nights. Lizards in this position are sometimes seen pumping their body up and down, as if they are doing push-ups. This behavior is a display for rivals or to claim territory or mates. They may look like they're resting in the sun, but lizards are also showing off their strength and size.

SKIN TIGHT

Like snakes, lizards shed their skin, but unlike snakes, they don't do it in one piece. Instead, as they grow, large flaps or strips shed off. Most lizards have dry, scaly skin.

HEATING UP

Well-adapted to its habitat, the chuckwalla can be out hunting even when the temperature tops 105° Fahrenheit. About one foot long with loose, leathery skin, this desert dweller eats plants and fruit. When threatened, it scurries into a rocky crevice and inflates its body like a balloon to avoid capture.

Special Talents

There are some remarkable lizards with distinctive qualities. The largest lizard, the Komodo dragon, can grow to 10 feet long and weigh as much as 300 pounds. Other lizards can be as small as a few inches long. Big and small alike, the world of lizards has some truly eye-popping members.

THE FEARSOME DRAGON

Named for its island home in Indonesia, the Komodo dragon is the world's largest lizard. Fast for its size, it can chase down animals such as deer or pigs and has no natural predators. These animals got the dragon part of their name from early European visitors who had never seen such creatures and thought they must be mythical dragons come to life.

PLAYING DEFENSE Some lizards use more than camouflage and speed to protect themselves. The shingleback skink in Australia has a tail that resembles its head. When threatened, it turns its body so the attacker doesn't know whether the animal is coming or going.

MAKING A POINT One look at the thorny devil shows the reason for its name. Sharp, pointed scales stick out in many directions from this Australian native. The devil "drinks" by gathering dew that collects on its body; its scale patterns direct the water to its mouth. Devils can eat more than 3,000 ants during a single feeding.

FLYING HIGH By expanding ribs and extending flaps of skin, flying lizards can glide through the air. There are several species with this ability. They live in the rainforests of Southeast Asia, so being able to move from tree to tree allows them to hunt and escape danger.

MONSTER VENOM The Gila (HEE-lah) monster is perhaps the most well-known venomous lizard species. Its powerful jaws grind toxic saliva into its victims; this venom can even be harmful to humans. The "monsters" live in the American southwestern desert and are the biggest lizards in the United States. New research has shown that other lizards, including the Komodo dragon, also produce venom.

A Colorful Display

The chameleon is famous for having the ability to change its skin into numerous colors. But it is not the only lizard that shows off amazing displays. Lizards change their skin colors to attract mates, hide from predators, or scare off potential rivals.

STICKY FINGERS

The fingers and feet of geckos give the animal a unique ability to stick to just about any surface. The bottoms of the feet are covered with tiny hairlike fringes that point backward. When the gecko touches a surface, even a wall or a ceiling, the hairs cling tightly and the gecko can anchor firmly and defy gravity. Geckos can even walk on windows.

LIVING COLOR

Lizards can be very colorful creatures. Their colors and patterns help them attract a mate and hide from predators

Five-lined Skink
Has stripes along the length of the body; stripes are blue at tail end.

Blue-crested Lizard
Found in the forests of China and neighboring countries, where it lives in treetops.

GREAT GECKOS

There are more than 2,000 species of geckos in a paint box of color schemes. Popular as pets, geckos range from less than an inch to more than a foot long. In the wild, they live everywhere from damp rainforests to woodlands to houses as pets. This tokay gecko gets its name from the sound it makes in its Southeast Asian home.

Oriental Golden Lizard
Male turns bright orange and red when it is trying to attract a mate.

Giant Ameiva
Frequently seen in South America; male has bright green skin on its back half.

Mwanza Flat-headed Rock Agama
Nicknamed "Spider-man" for its half-bright blue, half-red body.

TINY TEAMMATES

Tortoises provide a buffet for various finches. The birds eat ticks that burrow into the tortoises' skin. In fact, a tortoise will sometimes stretch its neck out in response to a "request" from a finch.

DID YOU KNOW?

The name of the islands is taken from an old Spanish word, *galápago*, which means saddle. Early Spanish discoverers of the Galápagos Islands thought the tortoises' shells looked like horse saddles.

GALÁPAGOS GIANT TORTOISE

Family: *Testudinidae*
Species: *Chelonoidis nigra*

The massive, slow-moving Galápagos giant tortoise is one of the rarest, yet most famous, members of the turtle family. It lives only on the Galápagos Islands, located in the Pacific Ocean off the coast of Ecuador. Different subspecies of the Galápagos giant tortoise live on several islands. Their differences, adapted for each island's food sources, helped Charles Darwin develop his theory of evolution during a visit there in the 1830s.

The Galápagos giant tortoise is thought to be the longest-lived animal on Earth; most live to be more than 100 years old, and one, named Harriet, lived to be 176. In fact, Harriet was collected by Darwin himself and lived until 2006. Tortoises can survive that long thanks to a lack of predators and an ability to go almost a year without needing to eat or drink.

The number of these tortoises that are alive today is only a fraction of the population that used to live on the islands. After the arrival of people in the 1800s, the population of giant tortoises on the islands plummeted. Four subspecies became extinct. The tortoises were hunted by sailors for their meat and by collectors for their shells. Rats from ships ate the turtles' eggs. By the middle of the 20th century, the population of the various subspecies had dropped from more than 100,000 to only a few thousand.

Since the 1970s, the government of Ecuador, which controls the islands, and scientists have strictly protected all the animals and plants of the Galápagos. The tortoise populations are now small but more stable, though the animals remain endangered.

Turtles and Tortoises

Turtles and tortoises have been around for more than 200 million years. There are more than 320 turtle species, and they all spend some or most of their time in the water. Sea turtles live their entire lives in the ocean. Tortoises live almost wholly on land.

STAR TURTLE

COMMON NAME

Galápagos Giant Tortoise

SCIENTIFIC NAME

Chelonoidis nigra

HABITAT

Grassland

LOCATIONS

Galápagos Islands

AVERAGE WEIGHT

600 to 800 pounds

FEEDS ON

Plants

Tortoise

WHICH IS WHICH?

Turtle or tortoise? Both are members of the order *Testudines*. Tortoises generally live only or mainly on land. Turtles usually live in or near salt water or freshwater.

Turtle

Shell Game

A turtle's shell sets it apart from other animals. Usually hard, the shell protects the turtle from predators. But there is more to a turtle than just its shell. The shell is attached to the turtle's body. It has four legs, a head, and a tail, too. When threatened or sleeping, the turtle pulls its head and limbs inside the protective shell.

REPTILE REPORT

Nearly all tortoises are herbivores; that is, they eat plants. Most turtles are herbivores, too, but some, such as the snapping turtle, are carnivores (meat-eaters). Turtle species that live in the ocean often eat fish and shellfish.

CHANGING TIMES

Tortoises have been hunted for their shells for thousands of years. Over time—due to hunting as well as environmental changes—tortoises became increasingly endangered. Conservation efforts on behalf of wildlife resulted in an international treaty—agreement between countries—that has the support of about 180 nations. Now, jewelry and other objects called "tortoiseshell" that are made or sold in any of these countries cannot be made of actual tortoiseshell. It is made of plastic designed to look like the natural material. You can find out more about the treaty and conservation efforts on behalf of tortoises and other endangered species at cites.org.

SHELL SECRETS

A turtle's shell is not one piece; it's a collection of interlocking and overlapping plates called scutes (SKOOTS). The top half of the shell is called the carapace (KARE-uh-pace). The bottom half is called the plastron. Turtle shells are not separate from the animal; the animal's vertebrae (spinal bones) are connected to the underside of the carapace. Skin and tissue are connected to the plastron, which surrounds the internal organs.

Snapping turtle

ROUGH: Jagged scutes stick out all over this type of shell.

Hermann's tortoise

DOMED: Shells of this type are high and rounded.

Smooth softshell turtle

SOFT: More like thick leather than hard plastic, these shells are usually found on water turtles.

GROWING UP TURTLE

Can a turtle outgrow its shell? No. The shell grows as the turtle grows. Smaller scutes are shed and replaced by larger ones as the shell gets bigger.

Turtles may generally look alike—a hard shell and a head and four feet sticking out. But among the more than 320 species, there is a wide variety of types. Turtles have adapted to many different kinds of habitats and can be found in areas around the world.

SNAP!

The alligator snapping turtle is powerful enough to snip off a human finger. However, its jaws are designed to catch fish, which are its main diet. This turtle's tongue is shaped like a small worm. The turtle lies still with its mouth open and wiggles the tongue as a lure to passing fish. Along with its powerful mouth, the turtle has a very distinctive shell. Large, jagged scutes fill the middle, while thorny plates ring the bottom edge.

TYPES OF TURTLES

From tiny sliders to massive land tortoises, turtle species offer a wide array of looks and a huge range of habitats.

Swamp:
Red-eared Slider
About a foot long; lives in wetlands throughout the U.S., Mexico, and South America.

Forest:
Yellow-footed Tortoise
At home on the floor of the forests and rainforests of the northern countries of South America.

STARRING ROLE

The Indian star tortoise has one of the most unusual carapaces. Each of the cones on its hard shell has a light-colored pattern that looks like a star. The cones are various sizes, giving this turtle's back the look of a mountain range.

Ocean:
Green Sea Turtle
Found in warm waters
around the world;

Desert:
Desert Tortoise
Digs into the soil of its
American desert home

Many Habitats:
Box Turtle
Found in most Eastern U.S. states;
habitats include woods, marshlands,

Everyone Into the Water

Most turtles spend some of their time in the water. But there are a few marine turtles that have adapted to live nearly their entire lives in the ocean. All of the seven species of sea turtle are listed as endangered. Populations around the world are battling pollution, climate change, habitat destruction, and overfishing.

HOME TO NEST

Sea turtles lay their eggs on beaches, burying them deep to protect them from predators. The turtles return again and again to the same beaches to produce their young. There are reports of leatherback turtles traveling more than 3,000 miles to find food after laying eggs, and then returning to the same beach once more. After hatching, the tiny turtles have to make their way into the surf, as shown above, where they are on their own in the big ocean. Conservation groups work to protect these nesting grounds from development so the turtles have a safe place for their eggs.

REPTILE REPORT

Are plastic bags killing sea turtles? Many coastal cities in the United States have begun banning plastic shopping bags. Scientists have shown that sea turtles eat the bags, possibly because they resemble jellyfish floating in the water. The bags can choke and kill the turtles.

MADE FOR THE OCEAN

Sea turtles have flippers instead of feet. This allows them to swim easily. They still have to surface to breathe, however. The largest turtle species is a sea turtle—the leatherback—whose name comes from its long carapace that looks and feels like leather. Like other sea turtles, it dives in search of food. Jellyfish are a big part of the leatherback's diet.

AMAZING RIVER TURTLE

In northern South America lives one of the most unusual members of the turtle order. The prehistoric-looking matamata lives its entire life in the rivers of the continent. It has a unique triangular head and a snorkel-like nose. It can wait for prey on the bottom of the river for hours, breathing through its "snorkel."

NILE CROCODILE

Family: *Crocodylia*
Species: *Crocodylus niloticus*

A visitor from prehistoric times spotting a Nile crocodile would feel right at home. These animals have lived almost unchanged for millions of years. Some fossils of this species have been dated at 3 million years old.

The Nile crocodile has probably survived for so long because its shape, size, and habits are perfect for its environment. The crocodile is the top predator in most of the river or swamp systems where it lives. A powerful carnivore, it can attack and devour almost any animal it comes across, from birds and fish to gazelles and even young hippos.

Nile crocodiles are the second-largest reptiles (after the saltwater crocodiles) and measure up to 20 feet long. They are easy to spot if their mouths are closed. There is a small notch along each side of the jaw, and a tooth sticks out of the notch on each side.

Mankind is the greatest threat to the Nile crocodile. Its range used to extend far north on the Nile River, but as its territory began to be developed, its numbers and range fell. Today, these crocodiles live on only a small stretch of the Nile River. However, their range has expanded across sub-Saharan Africa.

THE EGYPTIAN CROC GOD

In ancient Egypt, Nile crocodiles were part of everyday life, though a part that Egyptians tried to avoid. One of the ancient Egyptians' many gods was Sobek, the crocodile god, who oversaw the army and its warriors.

Crocodilians

Members of the crocodile family have changed little since prehistoric days, except that modern crocodiles are much smaller. Like their ancestors, crocodiles have hard, scaly skin and long snouts, and thrive in a watery environment.

This baby Nile crocodile basks in the sunlight, taking in the warmth.

PREHISTORIC CREATURES

When scientists call crocodiles "living dinosaurs," they're not exaggerating. Today's crocodiles are smaller than their long-ago ancestors, but their body shape and parts are similar to those of prehistoric crocodiles. One such animal was the *Sarcosuchus imperator*, nicknamed SuperCroc. It was more than 40 feet long and weighed more than 17,000 pounds. That's heavier than four family cars. Crocodilians were among the few reptile groups to survive the mass extinction event that killed the dinosaurs 65 million years ago. The crocodiles that live among us now descend directly from those survivors.

Crocodiles have five toes but only three of these have claws. The dinosaur who left this footprint had three toes—all with claws.

STAR CROC

COMMON NAME
Nile Crocodile

SCIENTIFIC NAME
Crocodylus niloticus

HABITAT
River, swamp, marsh

LOCATION
Africa south of the Sahara

AVERAGE LENGTH
12 to 18 feet

FEEDS ON
Fish, mammals, birds

Croc and Gator Basics

The name of this family—which includes the 23 species of crocodiles, alligators, and other similar animals—comes from a Greek word meaning "pebble." Indeed, the animals' rough, bumpy skin looks pebbly and scaly. Like other reptiles, crocodilians are cold-blooded. They spend a lot of their life in or near the water, so they need waterproof skin. Other than evolving to be smaller, crocodiles are among the animals least changed from prehistoric times.

WHAT'S THE DIFFERENCE?

An alligator (top) and a crocodile (bottom) are similar in shape and body parts, and both are crocodilians. Alligators have a stout, rounded snout (when viewed from above), whereas crocodiles have an elongated, thinner snout.

GOOD PARENTS

Unlike most reptiles, crocodiles spend a long time protecting their offspring. The eggs are laid in pits a short distance from water. After they are hatched, the mother guards the hatchlings from danger. When they are big enough, she carries them to the water . . . in her mouth. The young crocodiles stay close to the mother as they learn to hunt and survive on their own.

HOW CROCODILES EAT

For such a large animal, the crocodile can be quite stealthy. It slips through the water with just its nostrils and eyes showing, approaching prey and lunging for the kill. The crocodile's powerful jaws can exert more than 2,000 pounds of pressure, and its sharp teeth can grab and hold animals as large as zebras and gazelles. But it can't easily chew. Typically, the crocodile will hold the animal underwater until it drowns or spin it underwater in what is called a death roll, breaking its bones or ripping it apart in the process. Then, the crocodile maneuvers the prey into its mouth to swallow.

CLOSE RELATIVES

The caiman (KAY-man) and gharial (GARR-ee-ahl) are also members of Crocodyliae. They are similar in shape to crocodiles but have their own unique features.

Caimans live in Central and South America. They have V-shaped snouts, similar to those of alligators, and most species are shorter than crocodiles and alligators.

The gharial has a long, narrow snout. At the tip is a fleshy blob called a "ghara," a word that means "pot" or "pitcher" in Hindi. Critically endangered, it lives in India and some neighboring countries.

In an encounter with an unsuspecting person, an alligator or crocodile could easily harm or kill. But crocodilians are at greater risk from people than the other way around. In the American South, the American alligator is common in rivers and swamps where people like to fish or hunt, so clashes occur. In fact, the alligator is often the animal being hunted. Also, alligators are losing habitat as cities and towns expand. Some people regard all alligators as a problem; other people are working to ensure that alligators can survive in the wild.

THE ALLIGATOR BUSINESS

American alligators have been hunted for centuries. People eat their meat and use their hides to make luggage, shoes, and more. By the 1960s, this species was in serious danger of being overhunted. A hunting ban helped restore the population. Some states began farming alligators, creating ways to raise the animals in captivity for sale. Louisiana's Department of Wildlife and Fisheries says the alligator business in its state alone has been worth more than $700 million. TV shows follow alligator hunters, and alligator meat is available at restaurants in many areas of the country.

Unwanted visitor in backyard pool

NUISANCE GATORS

When alligators move into areas where there are people, the people get help. Professional alligator removers work all over the South, trapping and relocating alligators from golf course ponds, people's backyards, and public parks. Alligators have snatched pets from some yards. On rare occasions, people are attacked, too.

The saltwater crocodile is perhaps the most dangerous member of the family. It weighs on average 2,200 pounds, which makes it the heaviest reptile in the world. Numerous attacks on people have been reported in Australia, where there is a sizable saltwater crocodile population.

Most animal lovers have heard of reptiles in the snake, lizard, turtle, and crocodile orders. Two smaller orders of reptiles don't get as much attention, but they're just as much a part of the class of reptiles as those others. One has been around for millions of years, and the other's members are often mistaken for snakes.

REPTILE REPORT

The pink-skinned ajolote lizard lives in Baja California, Mexico. Unlike other worm-lizards, it has retained two of the limbs that the others have lost. Its digging skills have earned it the nickname mole lizard.

REPTILE RIDDLE

They are long and thin and, with some exceptions, have no limbs. They have scales, but the scales are in rings, not in rows as on snakes. They're not worms because they have a skeleton. What are they? They're Amphisbaenians (am-fiss-BAY-nee-ins), also known as worm-lizards. More than 140 species of these shy, slinky creatures live around the world and are part of their own separate reptile family. They spend nearly all of their lives underground digging for the insects that make up most of their diet.

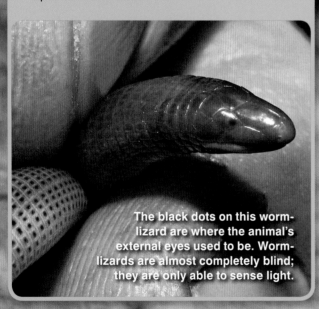

The black dots on this worm-lizard are where the animal's external eyes used to be. Worm-lizards are almost completely blind; they are only able to sense light.

DID YOU KNOW?

Tuataras seem to live their lives in slow motion. Unlike lizards, the tuatara does not reproduce until it is between 10 and 20 years old; lizards can do this much sooner— when less than a year old in some species. And tuatara eggs need as long as 15 months to hatch; most reptile eggs are ready in 90 days.

THE LONELY TUATARA

At a glance, this animal looks like a brown iguana, but it's different from its lizard look-alike in many ways. The only member of its order, the tuatara is not a lizard; and it is placed in its own family due in part to the shape of its skull, which has a beak like a parrot. It also does not have teeth but instead has a ridged jawbone. Dinosaurs called rhynchosaurs were its closest relatives. The tuatara is considered a living dinosaur. Fossils for this animal have been found that date back more than 170 million years; today's tuataras are nearly unchanged in all that time. All the wild tuataras in the world live on islands off the coast of New Zealand.

Tuataras are about 2 feet long and feed on birds' eggs and insects.

The process of discovering new animals is continual. Of course, those animals have been there all along. It's just that scientists have finally tracked them down in person. The other way of finding a "new" animal is that science has evolved new technologies and abilities to see differences in animals they once thought to be the same. Of course, in either case, it sometimes means trekking through miles of jungle or spending weeks in a remote place waiting for the new animal to come along. Through all that hard work, new reptiles are discovered every year in locations that are both out of the way and very close to civilization.

Anniella grinnelli was one of four new legless lizard species found in 2013. This one was named for Joseph Grinnell, a zoologist and founding director of the Museum of Vertebrate Zoology at University of California, Berkeley.

NEW SPECIES LANDS AT LAX

In 2013, scientists found a species of legless lizard in a very unusual place: next to a runway at busy Los Angeles International Airport, also known as LAX. DNA research proved that the "new" *Anniella stebbinsi* was actually one of four new lizard species in the *Anniellidae* family group the researchers had found in southern California. All were new subspecies of similar animals. Once they found they had new animals to name, they chose to honor respected herpetology experts; the LAX creature was named for biologist, conservationist, and reptile authority Robert Stebbins.

DOUG SAYS

The discovery of a new species of anything—be it plant or animal—is always an exciting event. Sadly, we live in a world where we are watching many species become extinct. And we suspect that a great many species that we have never laid eyes on are vanishing every day. Equally as thrilling is rediscovering a species that we thought had already gone extinct. That gives us a second chance to do right by this species. This rarely happens, yet when it does, it shows us that in some cases there is still time to correct our past environmental mistakes and that our planet still holds untold mysteries and discoveries after all this time.

—*Doug Hotle, Herpetologist*

Scientists have identified nearly 10,000 species of reptiles . . . but they know more are out there. Explorers, scientists, and reptile fans scour the Earth's hidden spots to find new species to add to the list.

IN HONOR OF . . .

Bothriechis guifarroi is a palm pit viper found in Honduras. The snake was named by its discoverer, Josiah Townsend, for Mario Guifarro, a local environmental leader who was killed doing work defending the rainforest.

A PEARL OF A FIND

Scientists studying turtles in the American South have known about the Pascagoula map turtle for decades. A similar turtle that lives in the Pearl River in Mississippi and Louisiana was assumed to be one and the same. After research by scientists from Northern Arizona University and a DNA test, it turns out they were different species. The Pearl River map turtle was announced as a new species in 2010.

SPIKY SEA SNAKE

Sea snakes glide through tropical waters, their smooth scales easing the way. A new species of sea snake found near Australia breaks that mold. The scales on *Hydrophis donaldi* each have a small spike sticking out, as shown in this photo. Scientists are not yet sure why the snake has the spikes.

FINDING A CROC

Matthew Shirley loves crocodiles. A researcher with the University of Florida, he thinks slogging through mud to find these amazing animals is a great way to spend a day. In 2014, his hard work made news. He and his team announced that they had found a new species: the slender-snouted crocodile. A Central African species had been known, but Shirley used his muddy research and DNA testing to prove a separate species.

How do you save a species? The key is understanding the threats. Are people hunting and killing too many members of the species? Are people destroying the animals' homes? Is disease or pollution harming their health? Is their food supply becoming limited? Once you understand what the problems are, you can try to figure out a solution. Here are some examples of how people are helping reptiles.

SAVING SNAKES

The herpetology curator at the Albuquerque BioPark in New Mexico is working to save a number of critically endangered species from that state. One particular snake, the Northern Mexican garter snake (*Thamnophis eques megalops*) was believed to exist only in small populations in Arizona and Mexico. Scientists had not seen the snake in New Mexico in more than 20 years. After three years of intensive searching, a team from the Albuquerque BioPark located a small population in the state in 2013. Doug Hotle is now studying this snake in the wild and has established a breeding program to help save this snake from extinction. It is very rare that scientists get a second chance to save a species.

Doug Hotle, herpetologist, taking accurate measurements of a Northern Mexican garter snake

DO NOT DISTURB
SEA TURTLE
NEST
VIOLATORS SUBJECT
TO FINES AND
IMPRISONMENT

TURTLE PATROL

More than half of the 320 species of turtles are under some sort of threat to survival. Sea turtles are in danger because their beach nesting spots are often in places where people use the beach, too. At a beach in Wrightsville, North Carolina, volunteers watch for new nesting sites. They keep the beach clear of trash that the baby turtles could eat; plastic bags are especially dangerous for sea turtles. When the babies hatch, the volunteers keep people and pets away so the turtles have a safe path to the sea. The Turtle Conservation Coalition writes, "It is now up to us to prevent the loss of these remarkable, unique jewels of evolution."

Nearly one in five snake and other reptile species is in danger of extinction. The good news is that scientists and communities around the world are fighting to save reptiles of all kinds. That work is called conservation.

Masaguaral Ranch in Venezuela is home to a private program working to increase the population of Orinoco crocodiles.

CROC COMEBACK

Seven of the 23 species of crocodiles are in danger of disappearing. One of these is the Orinoco crocodile, which lives in Colombia and Venezuela. Hunters killed nearly all of these animals for their skins to make clothing or luggage. At one point, experts believe there may have been only 250 Orinoco crocodiles left on Earth. Conservation has helped the animal come back. In Venezuela, more than 5,000 eggs have been hatched with help from people. After hatching, the babies (shown here), are put back into their river habitat. Crocodiles might look fierce, but they need help from people to survive.

People who work with snakes and other reptiles love what they do. It takes a lot of study and they all have to be very aware of the habits and dangers of these animals. But for people who want to be part of that world, there are many opportunities.

A **zookeeper** is an expert in a wide range of animals; reptiles might be just some of the animals he or she takes care of. Zookeepers make sure all the creatures at a zoo are safe and well-cared for. They also work with the public to help people enjoy and learn about the zoo's residents. Zookeepers study biology and other animal-related topics in college, but often learn "on the job" with internships.

A **veterinarian** is a doctor for animals. Most vets can treat any animals, but some specialize in working with snakes, crocodiles, and other reptiles. Reptilian veterinarians work with zoos, animals parks, and even pet owners, to ensure these creatures' health. Vets go through extensive training, including at least four years of school after college along with months or years of internships.

Animal habitats can be affected by people in many ways, from pollution to overcrowding to overfishing or hunting. Making sure that snakes, reptiles, and all animals have healthy habitats is the job of a **conservationist**. These people may be scientists who work with governments, private agencies, and the public to protect animals that are threatened. Conservationists try to solve those problems and help the animals thrive.

In laboratories and in the field, **researchers** try to find out more about reptiles. They study the animals and share what they learn with zookeepers and herpetologists. Researchers can discover new ways to help preserve species, and with snakes. for example, they can also find new antivenoms for snake bites or new ways that venom can help cure human diseases. Most researchers in this field have advanced graduate school degrees.

A **herpetologist** is an expert in all things reptile. Herpetologists study the animals in college and possibly in graduate school programs. Hands-on training at zoos and wild animal parks is another way they learn. Some of their work might be in education, teaching people about the animals. They might also work at a zoo helping to care for reptiles.

PAUL ROSOLIE
Conservationist and Rainforest Adventurer

The rainforest around the Amazon River in South America is home to more species of plants and animals than anywhere else on Earth. Paul Rosolie grew up in New Jersey, and he first visited Peru's Amazon rainforest when he was only 18. Since then, he's become an expert on the area and has focused his work on preserving its wild places.

"Rainforests were my childhood obsession," Rosolie said. "For as long as I can remember, going to the Amazon had been my dream. In my first ten minutes there, I heard the loud calls of howler monkeys. I saw trails of leaf cutter ants under impossibly large, vine-tangled trees. And a flock of scarlet macaws flew across the sky like a brilliant flying rainbow. It is the most amazing place on earth."

Discovery Channel recently started working with Paul as a snake expert based on his expertise with anacondas.

Paul's dedication to saving the rainforest and providing a safe home for millions of animals has led him deep into the Amazon basin. He's an expert on the mighty anaconda, the world's heaviest snake and a top predator in the Amazon. During one trip with a fellow guide to a huge lake there, he spotted an enormous anaconda he estimates was at least 25 feet long. "Snakes measuring over 20 feet are extremely rare," Rosolie says, "this one was a living legend. In future explorations, spotting her again will be one of my primary goals."

Another main goal of Paul's is to work closely with the people who live in the area to help safeguard animals. He studies with local trackers to truly know the ways of the rainforest and the creatures that live there. Paul also works hard to stop the illegal trade in exotic and endangered animals.

Paul loves sharing his passion for the animals and the area through his adventure travel company, Tamandua Expeditions.

By showing people the amazing places in the rainforest, Paul hopes to spread the word about how important it is to save and preserve these unique habitats.

Would you like to have fun with snakes and other reptiles? Here are some things that you can do at home or with friends— or you can ask your teacher about doing them with your class at school.

TAKE A WALK ON THE WILD SIDE

Find a wild place near you—a park, forest, meadow, riverside—and plan a walk with friends or family. Make sure adults are with you. Walking in nature is not like walking on the sidewalk. And remember what the reptile experts say: Treat every snake and other reptile as if it is dangerous. Never approach a snake or reptile. Enjoy it from a distance if you spot one in the wild.

HERE ARE SOME TIPS TO MAKE YOUR NATURE WALK SUCCESSFUL:

PLAN AHEAD. Talk to a park ranger or do research in your library. Find out what animals live in your area so that you can watch especially for them. Make sure you know the trail or route you're taking.

MOUTHS CLOSED, EARS OPEN. Listen for animal sounds, from skittering lizards to chirping birds. See if you can spot the animals making the sounds.

LOOK FOR CLUES. Do you see footprints? What animal made them? Can you find shed snake or lizard skin? Can you spot something an animal left behind, like poop? See if you can figure out which animal left it.

TAKE NOTES. Bring a notebook with you to record what you see, hear, and smell. Keep an eye out for things that change from walk to walk, depending on the weather, time of year, and time of day.

CLICK! Don't forget a camera to take pictures of what you see. Remember this nature saying:

Take only photos; leave only footprints.

MAKE A SNAKE

Draw your favorite snake, or imagine what a brand-new species might look like. To get started, ask yourself some questions to help you decide how your snake will look and act.

- ➡ What **SHAPE** will the head be: triangular, round, or elongated?
- ➡ Will its **SCALES** be smooth or rough, big or small?
- ➡ Does your snake have a thin or thick **BODY**? Is it long or short?
- ➡ What kind of **TEETH** or **FANGS** does your snake have?
- ➡ What does it **EAT?**
- ➡ What is your snake's **HABITAT?** Does it slither through a grassy field, hide out among the leaves on the forest floor, wrap itself around a branch, or glide through water?

Here's what you'll need:
paper or poster board
crayons or markers.

Don't forget to give your snake a name!

DOUG SAYS

Keep a field notebook. I spend many days and weeks in the field looking for snakes I can help. My staff has helped to save several species in New Mexico. While working, I keep detailed notes. Make a field notebook of your own for your next hike.
—*Doug Hotle, Herpetologist*

MAKE A MOVE-IE

Different snakes move in different ways. Some slither in a straight line, while others undulate or move up and down to propel themselves forward. Some are sidewinders, and others move in a concertina motion, bunching up their bodies and then pushing forward. Get your friends together and imitate all these different snake movements, then make a video for your friends and family to enjoy.

HOW YOU CAN HELP

Reptiles need our help to survive and thrive. Kids can be an important part of the effort.

➜ **Join a cleanup day.** Reptiles live near beaches, rivers, ponds, and in nature parks. Local conservation groups stage cleanup days at these sites to pick up trash and clear habitats. With the help of an adult, look online for dates and times. Can't find a cleanup near you? Organize one yourself for friends or make it a family outing.

➜ **Start a kids' conservation club** in your neighborhood or school. Talk to kids you know, and think up ways to help raise awareness of reptile issues or money to donate to a conservation group doing important work. A group trip to your local zoo or nature preserve is a great way to get started. Children interested in animals can be great advocates for their survival.

➜ **Talk to your teachers** about inviting a reptile expert to visit your classroom to show some of the animals he or she takes care of. Find an expert through your local zoo or natural history museum or an exotic pet store. Many cities have clubs for owners of pet snakes or reptiles; they might love to show you their amazing animals.

PLACES TO VISIT

The best zoos have reptile houses or exhibits where you can see snakes, turtles, lizards, and more. Some of the places on this list even specialize in reptiles.

ZOOS AND AQUARIUMS

CALIFORNIA

San Diego Zoo
2920 Zoo Drive
San Diego, CA 92112-0551
zoo.sandiegozoo.org

This is one of the most famous zoos in the world, and it has many types of reptiles. See an anaconda, a king cobra, hundreds of lizards, alligators, and more.

San Francisco Zoo
1 Zoo Rd.
San Francisco, CA 94132
sfzoo.org

A large Komodo dragon is the highlight of this zoo's reptile population.

FLORIDA

Reptile Discovery Center
2710 Big John Drive
Deland, FL 32724
reptilediscoverycenter.com

It's reptiles only at this site near Daytona Beach. Alligators, snakes (including cobras, pythons, and boas), large lizards, and many more reptiles live here. The center also does a lot of work extracting venom from snakes—and you can watch!

ILLINOIS

Lincoln Park Zoo
2001 N. Clark St.
Chicago, IL 60614
lpzoo.org

Boas, caimans, lizards, turtles, and more live at this Chicago zoo. If you visit, ask about their work helping to protect the Eastern Massasauga rattlesnake. Many zoos work hard to protect animals in the wild, while using zoo animals to educate the public.

Shedd Aquarium
1200 S. Lake Shore Dr.
Chicago, IL 60605
sheddaquarium.org

A huge alligator, snapping turtle, and a mighty green anaconda are among the reptile highlights at this popular aquarium on Lake Michigan in Chicago.

KENTUCKY

Kentucky Reptile Zoo
200 L and E Railroad Place
Slade, KY 40376
kyreptilezoo.org

Visitors can watch experts extract venom from snakes that will be used in research and to make antivenom. Get your picture taken with an alligator and visit with a huge desert tortoise.

MASSACHUSETTS

New England Aquarium
1 Central Wharf
Boston, MA 02110
neaq.org

Wind your way up around the unique corkscrew shape of the New England Aquarium's giant tank. Green sea turtles swim there, and you can see a huge green anaconda in the Amazon rainforest exhibit.

NEW MEXICO

Albuquerque BioPark
903 Tenth St. SW
Albuquerque, NM 87102
http://www.cabq.gov/culturalservices/biopark/zoo

This is home base for Doug Hotle, the SNAKEOPEDIA reptile expert. Visitors can see Doug in action and also get acquainted with Komodo dragons, mambas, rare Chinese alligators, and dozens more endangered and rare reptile species.

NEW YORK

Bronx Zoo
2300 Southern Boulevard
Bronx, NY 10460
bronxzoo.com

Visit the World of Reptiles at this world-famous zoo. Special exhibits highlight reptile camouflage and a reptile nursery. Plus see Galápagos tortoises.

SOUTH CAROLINA

Edisto Island Serpentarium
1374 Hwy 174
Edisto Island, SC 29438
http://www.edistoserpentarium.com/

Located south of Charleston, this reptile center is home to dozens of animals, many personally collected by the Clamp brothers who founded the center.

SOUTH DAKOTA

Reptile Gardens
8955 S. Highway 16
Rapid City, SD 57702
reptilegardens.com

This is the home of dozens of the deadliest varieties of snakes. The family that opened it in 1937 still runs it today. Several of the animals that live here have been used in movies and TV shows.

TEXAS

San Antonio Zoo
3903 N. St. Mary's Street
San Antonio, TX 78212-3199
sazoo-aq.org

From African rock pythons to yellow-footed Amazon river turtles, this zoo boasts a large reptile collection. SNAKEOPEDIA expert Doug Hotle recommends a visit to see the rattlesnakes, pit vipers, skinks, tortoises, and more.

WASHINGTON, DC

National Zoo
3001 Connecticut Ave NW
Washington, DC 20008
nationalzoo.si.edu

The Reptile Discovery Center at this zoo in the nation's capital features more than 70 animals, with several hands-on exhibits to learn more about snakes, lizards, and more.

CANADA

Indian River Reptile Zoo
2206 County Road #38
Indian River, ON
K0L 2B0
Canada
http://reptilezoo.org/

This large park features more than 200 reptile species. Along with reptiles of today, Indian River is home to a large dinosaur fossil collection and a display of dinosaur models.

EVENTS TO ATTEND

Repticon
repticon.com

Reptiles of all sorts come to a town near you at Repticon. Visit the website to find a show in your area.

BOOKS TO READ

The New Encyclopedia of Snakes
By Chris Mattison

This book provides detailed information about snakes, and shows hundreds of snake photos, including some of very rare species. Considered a definitive guide to snakes, *The New Encyclopedia of Snakes* is a good resource for anyone looking for information about snakes.

Mother of God: An Extraordinary Journey into the Uncharted Tributaries of the Western Amazon
By Paul Rosolie

Mother of God chronicles Paul Rosolie's adventures in Amazonia and the beauty of the threatened wildlife that lives there. Geared to young adult and adult readers, this true adventure story tells of dramatic encounters with giant anacondas and jaguars, and takes readers into one of the wildest places on earth.

Awesome Snake Science: 40 Activities for Learning About Snakes
By Cindy Blobaum

A hands-on book of activities, projects, and games that are based in science, including many snake facts.

Smithsonian Handbook: Reptiles and Amphibians
By Mark O'Shea and Tim Halliday

Designed as a sort of field guide, this book features short entries on hundreds of reptile species, along with a section about the amphibians that live not far from reptiles on the animal family tree.

Snakes: A Golden Guide
By Sarah Whittley

This pocket-sized guide will be good to take along on nature hikes. Most of the images are drawings rather than photos; the text gives a quick overview of snake families around the world.

ORGANIZATIONS

The Reptile Database
reptile-database.org

Packed with information, this site is maintained by reptile experts from around the world. They collectively update it with new information so it is always changing, from the number of species listed to how much information is available for each.

The International Union for the Conservation of Nature
iucn.org

The International Union for the Conservation of Nature (IUCN) is a global environmental organization. Their "Red List" of endangered species is updated often to show which species are facing trouble. You can visit their website to see how your favorite reptiles are doing.

World Wildlife Fund
wwf.panda.org

The World Wildlife Fund (WWF) is an important animal conservation organization. Their website includes lots of information on marine turtles and their fight for survival in the world's oceans.